I wish to dedicate this book to my deceased colleague, Recruit Garda Gary Sheehan, who died in a tragic shoot-out in the line of duty at Derrada Wood, Ballinamore, Co Leitrim on 16th December 1983. Gary should have lived to enjoy serving the community and bear witness to similar work experiences as recounted in this book, but it was not to be.

To Detective Sergeant Enda Moore, colleague and close friend, who probably had more bizarre work experiences than I ever had. Enda died unexpectedly, aged 47, and is still dearly missed. Enda taught me not to take myself and the job so seriously.

To Detective Neil Mc Manus, my last work partner/friend before I retired. He spent most of his time having a laugh at my expense. Neil is still out there fighting crime. I taught him everything he did not need to know about policing!

Finally, to my dear friend, Walter Marx, whom I met in hospital, literally by 'accident,' many years ago and who has kept in regular contact from America over the years. He is a most interesting and intelligent businessman who still works into his eighties and has written a book about his life. Walter told me I could write, so blame him if you do not like this book!

FOREWARD

'The Guard' was a hit film depicting the often mundane, bizarre, but occasionally fascinating life of a rural policeman. Brilliantly acted by Brendan Gleeson it offered viewers an insight into the daily happenings in towns, villages, backwaters and homes across the western seaboard.

The 'border' was a tough assignment for the new recruit writer of this book, Garda Cyril Meehan.

One of his close friends, Garda Gary Sheehan (23) was shot dead by the IRA in woods at Ballinamore, Co Leitrim, during the shoot-out to rescue supermarket tycoon, Mr Don Tidey.

I first met now retired Garda Sergeant Cyril Meehan over 25 years ago. As a 'cub' reporter on the *Donegal News*, where I now work as Deputy News Editor, Garda Meehan was a flamboyant, charismatic 'cop' who, more often than not, had a 'good case' in the courts. He also had a 'nose' for what might make a good read.

Depending who you talked to, Detective Sergeant Cyril Meehan was loved and loathed almost in equal measure. Sergeant Meehan was a no nonsense type. If a job had to be done, he was first to put the hand up.

A typical Donegal Saturday night would see an influx of up to 2,000 raving youths into the town. It was no place for the faint-hearted or easily offended, but with scant resources the local Gardaí met the challenge head on and did their best to keep the peace.

Over the years, the Garda Commissioner commended Garda Meehan for good police work 21 times. Garda Meehan also received a bravery award. He spent his final Garda years in Donegal as Detective Sergeant in the Regional Crime Unit.

Off-duty, many Gardaí got involved in sports, community, voluntary and musical groups. They plied their trade with the motto 'prevention was better than the cure'. Few kids who kicked a ball around Letterkenny in the 80s wouldn't have known a few Gardaí at the time.

Sergeant Meehan was a zealous officer, sometimes, maybe a little over–zealous! He will forever be remembered as the local Garda Sergeant who made a call to a pub enquiring about late hours to find when he pushed open the door it was a building site!

He has collected and documented in this book a unique and priceless collection of funny incidents that happened in the force over the years.

I will forever remember him driving carefree around the town in his distinctive red coloured Morris Minor.

Today, Cyril is enjoying life in Newport on the Greenway from Westport to Achill Island. He is a great storyteller and raconteur. I'm sure you'll read his book with as much fervour as I enjoyed his company. A Garda he was, but a friend he still is.

Charlie Joe Mc Ginley
Deputy Editor
Donegal News

INTRODUCTION

Coming from a strong tradition of policing it was almost inevitable that I would follow in the footsteps of my father, uncle and grandfather. All I ever wanted was to be a policeman.

My father was a policeman for almost forty-three years and must have, throughout that time, witnessed many more funny incidents than I. A reserved man, he was an excellent conversationalist on a one-to-one basis. When he retired he was interviewed on local radio about his career. He was less comfortable in this type of situation than that of natural conversation on the street. He was somewhat 'stumped' when asked if he had any interesting or funny stories to tell the radio listeners.

I remember thinking at that time that when I retire I would make sure I would remember and document as many of my experiences as possible.

I served thirty years in An Garda Síochána, was transferred on eleven occasions and worked in border stations during 'the Troubles,' cities, large towns, rural stations and islands. I worked in the uniform section, offices, teacher training and detective undercover work in the northwest, southeast and east of Ireland.

I retired as a Detective Sergeant in 2013, full of pride knowing that I was formally commended for good police work over 20 times, saved seven lives and was awarded for bravery.

I will not say that I never did anything wrong or regrettable, but if I did I escaped without being caught or disciplined!

Many Gardaí could tell more interesting and exciting stories than mine, but unfortunately most have not written about them. Most of the time police work is far from being funny. The world has become faster and crime more serious, and there is even less time for police to savour the humorous side of interacting with people in their work. Many officers feel more comfortable telling such stories to colleagues and friends in private. I was one of the few who took note of most of my stories when they occurred, to ensure I did not forget!

To the cynics who love to put policemen and women down, I say come back and look straight into an officer's eye when you have: been involved in risking your life; saving life; comforting crime victims; breaking bad news to people; been threatened; your family threatened; your personal property damaged; been assaulted on and off duty; been threatened by influential people with transfer because you did your work diligently; your every action under scrutiny; to make split-second decisions that could cost you your career, your liberty or life; been tarred with the same brush as colleagues you might not even know personally, who were detected for wrongdoing.

The next time you see that Garda in uniform consider that behind that official appearance lies a human being with attributes and failings like everyone else. He or she might have great stories and experiences to share, if only given the opportunity.

You might conclude after reading this book that Gardaí do nothing more than go around wasting time and taxpayers money enjoying themselves instead of fighting crime! For every funny incident in a thirty-year career, any Garda could give multiple accounts of horrific, dangerous and traumatic events they had been involved in or witnessed. All that said, life is serious enough most of the time, so lighten up and read these stories that I hope you enjoy.

Welcome to my account of some of those stories. Bain sult as!

THE IDEAL GUARD

(My father had a copy of this poem. He did not know know who wrote it.)

His back is straight, his head erect, his shoulders square and strong.
When he is around, you may be sure, there's little will go wrong.

He's shaven clean, his hair is trimmed, he's always neatly dressed,
His footwear really glitters and his pants are neatly pressed.

He always gets things done on time, he's never, never late.
His middle name is modesty – he has never heard of hate.

He studies much and listens well and seldom makes comment.
He's sweet of temper, rich in grace and always seems content.

He's brief, concise and legible in writing a report
And it's great to hear him give his evidence in court.

His dealings with the public are with tolerance and tact.
When speaking, he consistently confines himself to fact.

A mine of information and in truth it may be said,
He doesn't have to write it down – he's got it in his head.

The Guide, the Code, the Circulars, the gents behind the bars,
The special weekly supplements, the list of stolen cars.

The hordes of travelling criminals, the local VIPs,
The doctors, vets and clergymen, suspicious absentees.

And in the great promotion race, he's not obsessed by pride.
When others wish to pass him out he meekly stands aside.

He's one of nature's gentlemen, this member strong and tall,
A paragon of virtue – an example for us all.

I owe this man my gratitude, to him I feel a debt,
And though I have sought him many years,

I HAVE NOT MET HIM YET!

Index

CHAPTER FOUR - LAUGHTER AT THE EXPENSE OF THE PUBLIC WE SERVE

CHAPTER FIVE - WHEN THE CUSTOMER HAS ONE UP ON THE POLICE

CHAPTER SIX - GETTING THE BETTER OF THE CRIMINAL AND PRISONERS

CHAPTER SEVEN - COURT CASES AND JUDGES

CHAPTER EIGHT - BIZARRE GUBU STORIES

CHAPTER ONE
THE LAUGH IS ON ME

I guess that if one is to have a laugh or recall bizarre stories at the expense of the public, colleagues, judges or criminals, it is only right and fitting that the author includes himself in the mix.

As the saying goes,

"If you cannot take it, don't give it!"

THE MAGICAL LIQUID READER

In Garda Headquarters, Phoenix Park, Dublin, opposite the Zoo, there is a small stone building nestled amongst a number of modern buildings called 'The Hospital.' Since the foundation of An Garda Síochána in 1922 every applicant for An Garda Síochána had to be examined there to check if they were medically fit for service. It remains the case to this very day. It is now run professionally by a team of doctors and nurses. Thirty years ago however, when I attended the hospital to be examined as a potential recruit, the staff who assisted the Garda doctor were not nurses but older, semi-retired Gardaí. They would do the basic preliminary tasks such as measure and document your height and weight, and arrange for candidates to give a urine sample.

To fail this medical process was to prohibit a career in policing. When I presented myself at the hospital back in early 1983 along with ten other candidates as a potential recruit the old guard gave me a round shaped glass container, similar to what you would find in a science laboratory and said,

"Fill that up."

I lined up with the others at the single toilet available and eventually delivered and handed back the sample. The old Guard lifted the sample, put it up to the window and shook it about in the container. In a very serious tone of voice he said,

"Meehan, I see your father is a Garda Sergeant!"

The ten candidates, all nervous 'green horns,' including myself, were momentarily dumbstruck with such a marvellous, mystical, scientific analysis that this man could perform from simply looking at a container of liquid.

He had just successfully taken the p*** out of us, in more ways than one!

14

In truth, my father had rung earlier inquiring if I had passed the medical. The 'p*** taker' made good use of the information he had acquired as a result of talking to my father on the phone.

This was to be my first encounter with Garda 'blue' humour and a lot more was to follow throughout my thirty years in the service...

ROAD BLOCKS

Back in the early eighties at the height of the troubles in Northern Ireland, I was an inexperienced but enthusiastic Garda recruit working along the border. A colleague and I were ordered by radio one night to immediately set up a checkpoint at Bridgend, which is along the border with Derry city. We were told by our supervisor that a patrol car was in pursuit of a car heading in our direction from Letterkenny.

Within minutes we had strategically placed our patrol car across the middle of the road and activated the flashing roof lights. We stood out on the road in anticipation. We quickly realised that if the car being pursued did not want to stop, it could easily get around the patrol car because the road was too wide. This was before the introduction of the 'stinger' device which can puncture the tyres of a car.

At the side of the road I saw a large number of building blocks and without hesitation, lifted them onto the road to make a barrier to cover the gaps either side of the patrol car. After a little while I had successfully made a makeshift *'Berlin wall.'*

We waited for the sound of roaring engines and sirens, but it was not to be. What an anti-climax when two cars eventually approached our location. They were travelling at no more than 30 miles per hour. The two cars stopped. They did not have much choice. It turned out that the second car was an unmarked patrol car with detectives. They did not get out of their car. Instead, over the radio system, they asked us to search the other car. The driver of that car turned out to be no other than a very prominent republican still very active in politics to this day. Although he said little and appeared unimpressed, he was completely co-operative.

We searched the car thoroughly and found nothing. We allowed it to get through the checkpoint by moving the patrol car out of the way. My over enthusiastic 'road block' measures did not pass unnoticed. The following week a Derry newspaper somehow got details of the incident and covered the story with jest.

These days, opposition politicians and media interviewers try to press this republican politician on his possible association with various IRA 'activities' in his past life. If given the opportunity, I too would question this political activist now wearing a suit,

"Were you at any point in the past, involved in ... leaking to the media, the story of my over enthusiastic road blocks?"

And More Signs Of The Times

An illustration of the neglect the good old Gardai have suffered in recent times was shown when on Thursday night last week, they set up a checkpoint at the Bridgend round-about. The poor lads whose squad car was parked on one lane were reduced to dragging builders blocks from the side of the road and placing them across the other lane to ensure that drivers observed the checkpoint. Sophisticated eh? Next week they might get the "Stop — Garda Checkpoint" sign, which is under repair, back.

17

KEEP AN EYE OUT

In a sleepy rural village there was but one single pub. While on patrol really late one night we passed the place. Judging by the number of cars outside it was obviously still open, in breach of the liquor laws. My colleague, Garda John Vaughan, and I decided to inspect.

Most public house window curtains are usually of very thick material, almost like black-out curtains that were in houses during the blitz in London in World War II.

Some cynics would have you believe that the reason pubs have such curtains is to bluff passing Gardaí into thinking that there are no lights or after-hour business going on inside. I am sure that's not true, right?

When we walked towards the closed front door I could see the firmly closed curtains had a breach of security, in that there was a gap still open. It was possible to see clearly inside the premises through the two badly joined-up curtains. I peeked in through the gap in the curtains and lo and behold, to my horror, the bar owner was blatantly pulling pints behind the counter and speaking with a large audience of customers around the bar. Nobody appeared to be suffering from dehydration or thirst!

I banged on the door and in an official voice said loudly,

"Gardaí on public house duty."

Time passed and you could hear the usual drop in voice levels, the shuffling like a herd of cattle and then, the deadly silence. For several minutes, there was no reply and eventually, after persistent heavy banging on the door, it opened.

"Come in Guards," said the owner, *"the place is empty!"*

Sure enough, I could see through the haze of cigarette smoke that the place was indeed empty. Through a frosted-glass rear window which led to an enclosed yard I could see the silhouette of customers. A man's cigarette glowed every time he took a puff from it. I tried to open the rear door, but it was locked. I asked the bar owner for the key to the door, but he replied unconvincingly,

"Sergeant, I do not know where that key is. Sorry."

The inspection of the premises was rapidly descending into a farce and it was about to get worse. I said to the bar owner,

"Look, never mind the key to the door. Sure I can see people smoking through that window and anyway, I saw them with my own two eyes in here a while ago, through the gap in those curtains."

The bar man suddenly became furious and shouted into my face:

"At least you have two eyes!"

He then proceeded to pluck one of the eyes out of his head and placed it on the bar counter, amongst the unfinished pint glasses.

My colleague and I looked at the prosthetic eye on the counter. We did not know whether to burst out laughing or leave the bar immediately, regretting ever going in.

To this day I do not know if the bar man incorrectly thought I was making fun of him with my saying,

"I saw it with my own two eyes,"

or maybe it was his tactic to shock us or to gain sympathy.

Needless to say the incident never ended up before the judge. It would have been laughed out of court. Can you imagine if I had said to the bar man, as I departed that night,

"I will have to keep an eye on this place from now on!"

LIGHT FOOTED

From time to time as part of policing Arranmore Island off the Donegal coast, I went there with the patrol car on the ferry and stayed overnight in a local B&B after night duty finished. The duty was mainly to provide a visible policing presence for the community and to prevent possible late night disorder and late night drinking in the pubs.

One evening I took the patrol car to the island on the last ferry of the day, as was the norm. I was not yet in uniform and went straight to the B&B where I had an evening meal and spent a couple of hours watching television before getting into uniform and taking up duty.

When that time of night came, I got into my uniform shirt, tie, jumper, jacket, trousers, dark socks and ... eh! Where were my official black shoes?

"S***!" I thought. "I forgot to bring my uniform shoes!"

I had been wearing bright white sneakers with even brighter blue florescent stripes on the sides of them as my off-duty dress. I could not be wearing more visible, non-regulation uniform shoes. What was I to do?

I felt a right fool and knew that the islanders would consider me eccentric, if not completely bonkers mad if they saw me in such irregular uniform attire. Innovation, however, is the mother of invention, as I decided to take my black socks off and wear them over my bright shoes, to 'mask them' as it were.

I got into the patrol car very quickly after dark before anyone could see me and started my patrol around the island. The word was out on the island that the Sergeant was about and the pubs were braced for my inspection. By the end of the night however, everyone was asking where the Sergeant was as he had not called to any bars. The following day I heard back from someone on the island that the local talk was all about what the hell the Sergeant was doing on the island for the night. It was speculated that there must have been something very big going down and he was too busy to deal with mundane basic duties like inspecting pubs!

In truth, my biggest fear all that night was that someone would come up to the patrol car and ask me to get out and deal with something. I often thought afterwards that if someone had come up to me and said there was a serious disturbance, a fight or even a murder scene for me to respond to, I would have had to say to the person,

"Ah, not to worry, it will work itself out!" and drive off at speed.

A SUCKER FOR THE LADIES

I answered the phone at work one day and included in my greeti ng,

"How can I help you?"

A sexy female voice replied slowly,

"I am the one who can help you!"

I laughed, thinking it was a colleague pretending to be a member of the public so I said,

"Go on, who do you really want?"

The reply was again in a slow sexy voice,

"It is you I want."

At this point it was getting a bit wearing so I said,

"You are all talk and no action," and hung up the phone.

The phone rang again and it was the sexy voice on the other end.

"Are you the man who said I was all talk and no action?" she enquired.

"I am," I said.

"I am not all talk and no action, I am all tongue and action," she replied quick as a flash.

In a humorous manner I tried to engage her in conversation in an attempt to identify her or establish whether she was mad, drunk, on drugs or a combination of all. This all ended with her telling me to meet her outside the town Post Office, at 11am the following day.

I logged the call in the Incident Record with the vaguest of details, knowing that colleagues would read it when briefing themselves at the start of later tours of duty. I particularly expected my Sergeant would want to know in minute detail the exact content of our conversation when he started work the next day.

The following morning my hunch was to prove entirely correct. The Sergeant came into my office on some trumped up mission. I was hell bent on making it difficult for him to get any sordid detail from me.

"Well... Cyril, you were working on the phones last night?" he asked in a friendly manner.

"I was, Sarge," I said.

"All quiet?" he asked with expectation in his tone.

"Indeed it was, thankfully," I said in a played down, bored tone of voice.

"So nothing unusual at all?" he pushed further, slightly impatient at this point.

I knew I had to tame him down so I decided to lead him on a little.

"Ah, the usual, a disturbance at a house up the lane, a couple of public order arrests and a traffic accident."

"And that was it?" he asked in a less than pleased voice.

"That's about it," I said, back in the routine bored tone of voice. I had him. He could not hold out any further and I could not stall him at this pace for much longer.

"*You had a call from a lady, I believe?*" he asked anxiously.

"*Some bird, that's for sure, Sarge,*" I replied, grinning and shaking my head from side to side, teasing him.

"*And she had a lot to say for herself?*" he said, by now in a barely controlled angry voice.

"*She certainly did,*" I tortured him further.

"*So, she was quite explicit then?*" he asked, trying to tease me out further.

"*That's putting it mildly, Sergeant!*" The dam could not hold any longer!

"*What the hell did she say?*" the Sergeant exploded.

In the shortest summary I could summon, I said,

"*She wanted to lick and suck something and it was not a lollipop!*"

The Sergeant's face got red before it creased into a grin. He chuckled uncontrollably with his shoulders going up and down, and his hands in his pockets playing with his change. He turned and left the room, obviously satisfied with the edited and limited 'titillation' I had given him.

Can you imagine the said Post Office at eleven o'clock that morning? It was the most secure and policed place in the country, as no doubt, curious swarms of Gardaí attentively patrolled the area in helicopters, horseback, patrol cars and foot patrols, all hoping for a look at the 'lollipop' lady!

PROTECTING THE PRESIDENT OF THE USA

It was 1984 and I was only a policeman for about a year when I was handpicked for an assignment to protect Ronald Reagan, President of the United States of America. Well, okay, actually, half of the entire Irish police force was also picked! In those days VIP security methods were cumbersome and often involved a no more strategic deployment of resources than saturation policing, pouring hundreds of Gardaí around the Presidential visit to Ireland.

President Reagan and his wife, Nancy, spent a summer's night at the beautiful Ashford Castle, outside Cong in Mayo, as part of their visit to Ireland. Gardaí were drafted in from all over the country and the area around Cong and Ashford Castle was swarming with bored Gardaí. Some were out on the roads, others around the outskirts of the castle, but most were stuck in ditches and hedgerows. I pulled the short straw and was unfortunate enough to be sent to one of the small islands on the lake right beside the castle. It was obviously to prevent frogmen or snipers from getting to our VIP by using the lake.

Garda Walsh and I were sent to one of these islands by boat and we were each given a small bag containing an apple, a chocolate bar and a mineral. These were our total survival provisions on this little island for the night.

The insects and midges quickly welcomed us for a couple of hours, eating us alive, until a summer rain shower and nightfall got rid of that problem. There we were, both of us sitting on a big tree log, bored and trying to entertain each other in conversation.

Later, when I went to relieve myself, I realised the tree I was behind was completely rotten. Although it still had a healthy looking bark exterior, it was totally rotten and soft as a champagne cork.

26

As the night wore on it got cold and wet. My jungle survival skills came to the fore when I told my colleague to remove his long waterproof coat. I buttoned his waterproof to mine and with a few long twigs and branches fashioned a fine tent to give us shelter. That ended the rain going down our necks.

"It would be great to have a fire," said Garda Walsh.

I replied, pretending to be angry with frustration at our predicament,

"See that tree over there. I am going to knock it down and we are going to burn it."

He looked at me as if I was mad! We had no chainsaw or hatchet, I am sure he thought to himself. I got up, roared loud like Tarzan and ran at the tree. With arms and shoulder pushed forward I shunted the tree really hard and the massive thing completely toppled over. Even though it was twilight, I could see the pale, shocked, amazed, yet appreciative expression on my colleague's face.

We spent the rest of the night enjoying the comfort of a large fire under the cover of a makeshift tent.

That's how I spent my time protecting the President of the United States of America!

BREAKDOWN IN TRANSLATION

When a young Garda from Mayo is sent to Donegal on first allocation the most immediate and biggest hurdle to overcome is the different accents. The recruit has also to learn a new vocabulary of words, such as:

Up the Brea = up the road
A Wean = a child
There is going to be a handling = There is going to be trouble

The first day I patrolled Buncrana's streets a young man walking past me on the street and in a harsh, quick voice said,

"What about you mucker!"

I thought he was telling me to f*** off and replied in a cross confrontational tone,

"What about you too, you mucker!"

I now know that the translation means *"Hello."*

Another night I was on patrol with a more experienced Garda who had acquired a working knowledge of the Donegal accent. We walked past a man with drink on him as he stood outside a pub. He asked me if I had a match, to which I replied that I did not smoke. My colleague almost bent over in laughter and there was a bemused if not confused look on the face of the man who had spoken to me.

I asked,

"What's the matter? What's so funny"?

My colleague just about managed to compose himself before replying,

"He did not ask for a match, he asked if you were... going to the match!"

It works the other way too! The natives sometimes do not understand the Mayo accent. I was on mobile patrol on the Port Road in Letterkenny one busy Saturday night. The street is a one-way system and I noticed a Northern Ireland registered car coming towards me in the wrong direction.

I rolled down the window of the patrol car and spoke across to the driver in the other car who had three passengers. I said to him in words to the effect,

"This is a one way street. Go back, you could have hit someone and you would end up arrested."

He looked at me and immediately complied by turning the car on the street before pulling in to the side pavement. I drove on and continued my patrol around the town. A number of times throughout the tour of duty I went up the same street again. I noticed that the Northern Ireland car was still parked in the same place and the passengers and driver were seated in it, looking at me anxiously each time I patrolled past.

I thought no more about it and continued my night's work. About three hours later I was back at base finishing duty and putting my uniform equipment away in my locker when a colleague shouted for me to go to the public office as someone had called to the station wanting to talk to me.

I went to the public office and there across the counter I recognised the driver of the Northern Ireland registered car standing there. I said,

"Can I help you?"

"Excuse me sir, but when are you coming back to arrest me?" he replied.

I did not know whether to laugh or cry for the poor individual, who had been so respectful and compliant to just sit there in his car for hours, awaiting arrest. All that this unfortunate Northerner obviously picked up from what I said in my Mayo accent was,

"I will be back to arrest you," rather than what I actually said, to go back the correct direction on the one way street and *"you could, (not would) be arrested if you had hit someone!"*

I can tell you from experience and many a car chase, a lot of young Northern Ireland motoring offenders would not be seen for dust as they would speed across the border to avoid arrest.

On the other hand, sometimes there is a distinct advantage in misinterpreting what someone says to you. A colleague of mine once got into an argument with another member over the phone about not carrying out a computer check for him. My colleague ended the phone conversation by telling the other member,

"You are nothing but a red-arsed recruit!"

This recruit was not impressed and reported my colleague over his abusive behaviour and mistreatment of a junior member. An investigation was carried out and my colleague was interviewed by an officer. My colleague avoided discipline as he was given the benefit of the doubt. He had protested in his defence that the recruit Garda had misunderstood what he had actually said.

He did not say he was *"a red-arsed recruit,"* but *"You are a recently arrived recruit!"*

YOU MUST BE KIDDING
OR JUST TRYING TO GET MY GOAT UP

Back in 1994 as a newly promoted, fresh-faced Sergeant, I was stationed in Burtonport fishing village in Donegal. Arranmore Island was also part of my area of responsibility.

The first day I visited Arranmore in uniform, I went on foot patrol of the entire place. The objective was to familiarise myself with the geography of the island, identify possible policing needs and get to know some of the people I was to serve. Maybe I was also going there to spread the message that there was a new 'Sheriff' in town!

After running out of road at one of the most remote parts of the island I came upon a small house with an old lady at the front door. As I passed she asked,

"Are you a Guard or a Postman?"

Somewhat bemused, I told her. She called me over and began whispering to me, which was not called for, considering there was not another human being to be seen within miles of this particular location.

"You have no idea what goes on around here at night," she said.

My police nose was itchy with interest as I asked,

"Really, like what?"

"Oh, the noise of the kids in the middle of the night, tormenting me with the banging and scraping of my front door," she said.

"Would you not consider telling their parents what their kids are up to?" I said.

The old lady's haggard face suddenly contorted into an expression of annoyance and obvious expression of despondency with what I had just suggested.

"No, no, you fool," she said, *"it's the kid goats I am on about, with them rubbing their horns against my door!"*

After advising her to maybe consider putting a nearby bonnet of an old car in front of the door at night to deal with the problem, I moved on smartly, asking myself if she was just 'kidding' me or trying to 'get my goat up!'

OPEN UP! I'LL HUFF AND I'LL PUFF AND I'LL BLOW YOUR HOUSE DOWN

Going down the main street of Letterkenny on inspections of bars and clubs one night at closing time, I found McClafferty's Bar diligently closed on time. The place was being renovated for some time but continued trading throughout the process. Convinced that there was drinking going on behind closed doors, I knocked the place up and shouted loudly a number of times,

"Garda on public house inspection."

There was no reply. Eventually I began to realise that just about everyone who was coming out of a nearby bar further up the street was laughing at me!

It turned out that the bar I was trying to get into was closed for complete rebuilding works. The entire building had, it appeared, been demolished behind the front door and wall, and was being propped up by steel pillars to prevent it collapsing. From the back of the premises

I later learned, it looked like one of those mock town frontages used in cowboy movies. Thankfully this was way back before mobile phones could video me and have the story go viral on You Tube or the like!

The incident may not have been captured on video, but it made no difference, as I was not let forget this hilarious embarrassment. All the regional newspapers covered the incident in the following days.

CHAPTER TWO
IN MY FATHER'S TIME

This chapter covers stories related to policing
before I even became a member.
Sometimes when asked how many years I served,
I reply, '50 years,' because from birth until I joined,
I was already surrounded by policing.
My father, grandfather, uncle and my immediate neighbours
were all in the police.

THE POWERS OF THE UNIFORM

My father was a Sergeant in the Gardaí and served proudly for over forty-two years.

I remember as a child going yearly to the bog with him to save the turf. The turf cutter, whom we called Jackie, always cut it in the traditional way. Jackie was a big strong man from a farming background. He had his own strange ways. When he went to town and drank he could become cantankerous and he was best avoided. One day in the bog my father noticed that Jackie's work coat was near to tatters, so, as an act of kindness he later gave him an old Garda uniform coat, minus the insignia and marked buttons. Jackie was delighted. My father was to later regret this act of kindness.

A few days later while at work in the Garda Station, my father received a radio message from a patrol car,

"Sergeant, you better come up here to Market Square. Jackie is in the middle of the road, directing traffic in your coat!"

WETTING THE TEA

When my father was promoted to Sergeant he was transferred to Castlefin in Donegal. It was during the troubles and this village, which was right along the border, had a large station party dedicated to dealing with the political troubles which were raging in the North. It was a standing order by the diligent new Sergeant that foot patrols would have to be carried out on each tour of duty, irrespective of the weather conditions.

It took over thirty years before my father was to learn that his batch of rookie Guards were not always as diligent as he thought. All those years later the story was told to me by a dear old lady when I was to meet up with her. The kind-hearted lady, who lived next door to the station at the time, was an 'accessory' to a Garda indisciplinary offence, so to speak. Not only did she conceal the supposedly patrolling Gardaí in the shelter of her home, she obliged them with a shower underneath her garden hose, before they returned to the station! After all, a Garda who had walked for hours in the rain could not return to the Sergeant anything less than drenched wet, could they?

GROWING CRIME IN WESTPORT

The old Garda barracks in Westport in Mayo was once located on James Street. Today, the old building is the site of a Social Welfare office and car park entrance. At the back of the then Garda station, where a large public car park has since been placed, there was a walled-garden which belonged to the local Garda station members. It was like those allotments that are becoming popular today. Each member had his plot and grew various crops of vegetables and fruit for their families.

My father had a spot in the garden and he grew potatoes, lettuce and rhubarb. The sheltered garden, with its high walls, had exceptionally good soil, so crops always grew well and were of good quality.

One day when I was about fourteen-years old I was in Seán O'Connor's Supermarket, then at the bottom of Peter Street. Seán was a great businessman and was always very kind to me. I was walking past his fruit and vegetables counter when I saw his stock of rhubarb on display. I shouted over to Seán, who was behind the meat counter,

"Seán, I can get you proper rhubarb, with stalks on them as thick as my arm!"

Seán told me that if I could get rhubarb as thick as my arm and tie them in bundles of four, he would buy some from me. I was so excited with my first business venture that I went straight to the barracks garden, pulled all my father's rhubarb and industriously baled them together with twine in lots of fours, as requested by Seán. I had them on the shelves of O'Connor's Supermarket before the day was out!

A few days later I was back in the supermarket when good old Seán came over to me.

"Young Meehan," he said, *"can you get any more of that rhubarb for me? The last lot all sold out. I will buy as much as you can supply."*

"Of course I can, Seán," I said with delight.

Down I went to the garden again. My father's entire crop had been taken by me at this stage, but that was not to prove to be an obstacle! Without hesitation, I cleared every other guard's plot of rhubarb and made my first 'million' out of Seán O'Connor!

To this day, the old retired guards in Westport still recall the year of the mysterious plant blight that overnight killed the entire barracks garden of rhubarb right down to the root!

I ONLY HAD THE 'ONE'

Many years ago there was a large seizure of illicit liquor, known to us as poteen (*poitín* in Irish), in a station my father served in. This type of detection usually took place just before Christmas, as this was the time of year the producer had the biggest stash, ready for the festive season market. The distilling vessels and worm used to make the product were taken to the local Garda Station.

More importantly, the barrels of the poteen itself were also seized as evidence. It was said that while at the Garda Station, the poteen had an unusually high 'evaporation rate.' It was suspected that some members had taken a drop of the liquid for 'medicinal purposes.'

After tests were carried out to confirm the content of the liquid for evidence, the poteen was to be destroyed in the presence of a local Peace Commissioner in accordance with regulation and best practice. My father, the Sergeant in charge of the station, on becoming aware of the imminent destruction of the poteen, asked the investigating member for a bottle of the liquid. I must add that my father was a proud holder of a Gold Pioneer pin (granted to those who have abstained from alcohol for fifty years!) He certainly did not want the poteen for drinking.

The member in charge of the case told my father that as there was so much 'evaporation' of the entire batch it would be almost embarrassing to present it before the Peace Commissioner who was to witness its destruction. He conceded however but was adamant that it could only be one bottle.

My father agreed with this, went down the town to a local pub and asked for one used whiskey bottle. He returned to the station, presented the bottle to his concerned colleague and said,

"You said one bottle, well there is one bottle!"

The bottle was one of those gigantic one-gallon (four and a half litres) whiskey bottles you seldom see today in pubs. That bottle was in a cupboard in our house for many years and anyone who suffered muscle pain or had an injured pet was given a sample from my father. It was mixed with linseed oil and some other 'mix' and was reported to be a magic cure.

UNDERCOVER SANTA IS FINALLY UNCOVERED

We all know, young and old, that there is only one Santa. However, as children we all believed for a time that the Santas in every shop or street corner at Christmas time were all real.

Kids eventually realised that there was only one Santa. My realisation of this came more abruptly and at a younger age than most kids.

Every Christmas, as a child, it was traditional for my parents to take the whole family to nearby Castlebar to do Christmas shopping, meet Santa and have fish and chips in an Italian restaurant/takeaway.

One year my father brought me up to Santa in his hut so I could sit on his knee and tell him how good I was and, more importantly, to list out all the toys I wanted from him on Christmas morning.

No sooner had I sat on Santa's lap when he excitedly shouted out,

"God, is that you Seán Meehan? Are you working over the Christmas?"

My father looked taken aback, until Santa quickly dropped his false beard from his face and said,

"Seán, it's me... Jack! How the hell are you keeping?"

My father immediately recognised his ex-Garda colleague and replied as they shook each other's hands,

"Ah, Jack, how is retirement treating you?"

There I was sitting on the knee of an impostor who had blown his cover, engaged in 'shop talk' and recounted old 'war stories' with my father, oblivious to the fact that it was the end of part of my innocence!

I think it would be fair to say that Santa Jack would never have been suitable for undercover police work at any point throughout his past career in policing!

CHAPTER THREE
FRIENDLY FIRE/BLUE ON BLUE

Similar to any other occupation such as a factory workers,
health service employees, firemen or soldiers,
police also, on occasions, deal with monotony,
boredom or the stresses of work.
The safety valve is often blue humour
at the expense of other colleagues.
This chapter covers such stories.

HORSING ABOUT

There had been several complaints by a head teacher about a number of caravans, some horse-drawn, that had taken up temporary residency outside the school. It was reported that some horses were tethered with rope from their legs to a timber stake in the ground immediately outside the school entrance. There was a fear that a horse might kick one of the children and the school was obviously worried about a breach of health and safety regulations.

Early one morning at work I answered a phone call from the school principal. The problem had not been resolved despite the Garda response and advice to the people in the caravans. The horses continued to be a threat. I told my colleague of the situation. His morning duty was to drive the marked patrol car and respond to calls.

"I am going to sort this once and for all," he said.

He left the station fuming with anger and I saw him walking fast and purposefully with clinched fists up the road towards the school. Time passed and I had almost forgotten about Garda Leydon's mission. Suddenly, in the quiet of the morning there was a loud noise, drowning out the only other sound, birdsong. It was the sound of horse hooves on tar. I looked out the window and there was Garda Leydon escorting a horse into the front car park of the station. I thought to myself that he had decided to seize the offending horse and was going to take it to the compound at the rear of the station.

I was wrong! Moments later, I could hear the loud echo of horse hooves again, this time louder than when I first heard them at the front of the station. The sound was coming from the long hallway – inside the station! Within seconds I saw Garda Leydon and the horse pass by my office through the glass door.

My mouth dropped and I shouted,

"Where the hell are you going with that?"

He replied,

"Give me the keys to the cell."

I thought I was calling his bluff when I gave him the keys, but it was not to be. He dutifully opened the cell and led the horse inside. Satisfaction written all over his face he came out of the cell, alone, and locked the door. Job done!

That particular morning I was the member in charge of the station, an onerous duty which included responsibility for calls to the station by the public and supervision of prisoners in cells. Half laughing, half worried, I said to Garda Leydon,

"You can't put it in there, it's not a prisoner!"

"It is now!" he replied.

Custody records are the 'Holy Grail' in policing. Members have to be very correct in making every entry into this custody log as they are often scrutinised minutely by defending solicitors and by judges in court proceedings. By now really worried, I thought I would bring this Garda to his senses.

"You will have to put the prisoner's details in the custody records so!" I said.

"Absolutely!" Garda Leydon replied confidently.

I was sure his bluff was now being called. Not a chance, as Garda Leydon commenced to fill in the custody log!

About this time, Garda Liam Canning arrived into the station. A Guard with long service and great experience, his first duty of the day was to let me go for breakfast for an hour. His perfect start to the day would have been a reply in the negative when he enquired if there were any prisoners in the cells. To have prisoners still in the cells was to make the start of his working day more complicated, as he would have the added responsibility of checking prisoners regularly and recording his activities in the all important custody log.

"Any prisoners in the cells this morning?" asked Garda Canning.

"Yes," I said to Garda Canning. *"One awkward bastard."*

"What is he in for?" Garda Canning asked despondently.

"Danger to children. Breach of the peace," I replied.

"The f***er," said Garda Canning as he grabbed the custody record to read the profile of the prisoner. He read each section aloud.

"Name and address: ... No reply, refused to give.
Date of birth: ... No reply. Won't talk.
So we have a smart arse," Garda Canning said as he read on further.
"Description: ... Big eyes, big ears, big nose and long face." He looked perplexed!

"*An ugly smart arse we are dealing with so,*" Garda Canning said.

He grabbed the custody record with enthusiasm and said to us as he went towards the cells to confront this prisoner,

"*Leave this one to me, I'll get the ugly, smart-arsed prisoner to give me his details.*"

"*Good luck with that one,*" I replied as I made a hasty exit for my breakfast!

49

EGG ON FACE

I once worked with a Sergeant who had a complete fixation about health and fitness. He analysed everyone he met according to their fitness, physique and body weight. Keeping himself in good physical shape included his eating very healthy lunches at work. You could set your watch by his routine at one o'clock each day at work. The salad would be prepared, the tea made and rested, the two eggs boiled. While the eggs boiled he usually resumed his office work for a few minutes, before returning to tuck in.

One particular day the Sergeant was preparing his usual lunch and put the eggs on boil. His office phone kept ringing as he was about to leave and he would have to race back up each time to answer it. Amazingly, the phone stopped ringing every single time he was about to pick it up. The Superintendent normally rang the Sergeant just before lunch, so the phone was responded to with more enthusiasm than any other time in the day.

What he did not realise was that one of my colleagues at work, who had the appearance of innocence and not capable of mischief, was actually the culprit in this story. He was in a nearby office and was tracking the Sergeant's every footstep on the floor upstairs. It was he who was making the phone calls to the Sergeant and then hanging up.

After running back and forth several times over several minutes, the Sergeant finally gave up paying attention to the phone calls and ran to rescue his, by now, very, very hard-boiled eggs. Just before he arrived back into the kitchen the innocent faced Garda beat him to it, whipped out the boiled eggs and replaced them with fresh ones, before silently and swiftly slipping away. When the Sergeant hit the eggs with the spoon, the raw eggs splattered all over the place. He could not understand how, after over ten minutes on full boil, the egg was still, completely raw!

TRUNK CALL

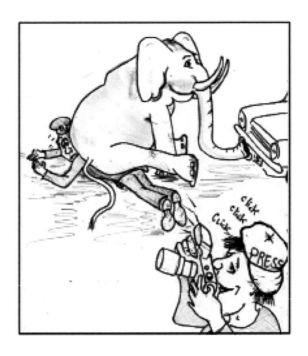

If you were in the police in Africa or India it would not be particularly strange, I suppose, for a police officer to get a report of an elephant blocking road traffic. If you were in New Ross in Wexford it would certainly raise an eyebrow or two!

The Gardaí at New Ross received a telephone call one day from a member of the public complaining about an elephant blocking traffic on the main New Ross/Wexford road. The Garda at the station immediately relayed the message to the patrol car by radio. After a long delay in replying, the crew in the patrol car responded on the radio in a tone of scepticism.

"Where did that report come from?"

A member of the public rang it in was the reply of the Garda at base. The crew of the car responded in a dismissive, sarcastic voice on the radio,

"Was that a trunk call?"

The Garda at the station got the pun alright but was not amused as he had received three further phone calls in the interim from other members of the public about the elephant. The car crew responded to the call and, true enough, there was an elephant in the middle of the road and traffic all over the place. The local media had arrived and started taking photos.

One of the Guards who went to the scene was very conscious of the media presence and about his image. He did not want to have the media take a photo of him trying to get the elephant off the road to the nearby compound belonging to the circus that had just arrived in the town. After some coaxing and the assistance of the circus elephant trainer, the elephant was taken away and traffic calm returned.

Back at the station the Garda who had been so careful to avoid being made a fool of by the media photographers boasted that he was cute enough to avoid such a fate. He triumphantly stated that he had made sure to keep right 'behind' the elephant at all times to prevent the photographers getting a shot of him with the elephant. Not to let the Garda think that he had been so smart in avoiding being ridiculed, it inspired me to create the attached cartoon, which circulated all over the station.

A GARDA TAKES POT

One time In Dundalk station there was a Guard who was famously known for his addiction to tea. He needed copious amounts of tea every day and could not function or make a decision on anything until he first had a hot cup of well-stewed tea.

Once, on night duty, he was taking a break from foot patrol along with other members back in the station kitchen. He whipped off his waterproof jacket and his utility belt that held all his work gear such as handcuffs, ASP baton, pepper spray, disposable gloves and radio holster, to make himself comfortable as he sat to his meal and his cup of tea. After a few minutes an urgent message cracked over the radios of all the members in the kitchen that there was a fight in progress down the town and other members needed assistance. Everyone in the kitchen, without a word, 'tooled up' immediately, whipped on their uniform jackets and clipped back on their utility belts before rushing out the door.

On the way to the disturbance in the 'paddy wagon' our tea-loving friend was wondering why all the other lads were laughing in the van. He looked down at his utility belt and realised that it had very recently acquired a new piece of essential work equipment! Someone had slipped something on his belt... a small teapot!

A GARDA 'HIGH ON GRASS'

While on mobile patrol through a residential area one summer evening, two Gardaí happened to see an off-duty colleague cutting his lawn at the front of his home.

The patrol crew could not believe their eyes and thought the sight before them was hysterical. Their experience of this individual at work was that he would, to put it mildly, never ever work up a physical or, for that matter, mental sweat. He certainly was a big advocate of the principle 'don't sweat the small or big stuff.'

In the weeks that followed, there were regular sightings of the same Garda seriously 'sweating' as he fought the good fight with nature. Inexplicably, his lawn was greener, always longer and needed cutting more regular than any of his neighbours. Hard as he tried, he was losing the battle against nature's growth.

Little did he know that, under the cover of darkness, his workmates returned to his house and liberally sprinkled fistfuls of agricultural fertiliser all over his lawn! The fertiliser improved the quality and speed of growth of the lawn alright ... tenfold!

SHREK

Many television viewers today are fascinated by CSI type forensic crime programmes. Such programmes are available on almost every channel. Criminals even admit to watching these programmes to learn how not to get caught for the crimes they commit. Not many people, however, have heard of one of the earliest forensic crime detection devices which was used back in the 50s and 60s in police work which is rarely used today.

This is the use of a powder called 'Malachite Green.' It is a fine, almost colourless powder which becomes a green dye when it comes in contact with moisture. It changes to dark green on activation and is temporarily impossible to wash off the skin.

Police used it mainly in investigations of theft where money was taken from church poor-boxes or where staff in a shop or factory were suspected of taking money or product from areas they should not have access to.

The powder is sprinkled on the money or product. When the culprit touches the money their hand moisture immediately activates the powder dye and their hands turn green. The more the hands are washed the greater the effect of the dye, which lasts for days on the skin. If police had a suspect, inspection of the hands often led to the case being detected!

There was this particular Guard who worked in a rural station and he was known to be very much the 'Scrooge' regarding money. He would use the station toilet paper and kitchen facilities to save himself money. He used the station shower rather than put pressure on his home immersion electricity bill. His work mates could put up with all this with a certain amount of amusement, but when he started using other members shower gel, it all became too much. It was the last straw.

One day while taking a shower at work 'Scrooge' gave himself a good scrubbing and lathered himself with green-coloured shower gel. As usual, it belonged to someone else in the station. Later, when he looked at himself in the mirror, he found himself looking something like Shrek, the film cartoon character!

He shrieked with shock at his new-found look. He was green in colour from head to toe. The more he scrubbed, the more the dye in the gel got darker. He was so embarrassed that he had to take holiday leave for a week!

Having time to simmer over his unfortunate incident at home, he finally realised what had happened to him and he promised to identify the culprit and wreak revenge. He commenced his investigation by ringing the forensic laboratory at Garda HQ as only they had access to and issued the powder to Gardaí for investigations.

"Has any of the powder been issued recently to my station?" he asked.

"Yes," came the reply.

"Aha! Now I'm getting somewhere," he thought to himself.

"And what was the name of the Garda officer at my station to whom it was issued?" he asked.

At this point he was relishing the moment when he would know the identity of his enemy, who would be taken to task for the heinous act inflicted upon his body.

"Eh ... it was your name on the application," came the reply!

For years afterwards, 'Scrooge' often had jibes from his colleagues with references to people being 'green with envy' and 'far away hills are green.'

When the new radio system was put in the door of all rural garda stations so people could speak to Gardaí at the local station headquarters it was nicknamed the 'Green Man.' The joke at 'Scrooge's' expense when new recruits came to the station on transfer was that they would be tasked with asking 'Scrooge' if the 'Green Man' (outdoor radio system) was working at the station. He always reacted the same, like the fury of the Incredible Hulk, while the recruit was left bewildered.

He never showered in the station again and the station electricity bill was lower, accordingly!

NO SLUMBER BECAUSE OF THE LUMBER

A colleague of mine took delivery of a full trailer of split timber blocks to the drive of his home for winter heating. As he was going to work for the night at the station he did not have time to put the fuel into his shed. It was to be something he would regret dearly the following morning when he returned home, weary and tired, from a long and busy night of work.

In the middle of the night when things became quiet, some of his colleagues happened to be cruising by his house while on patrol and copped the load of timber. They quickly rushed into the drive of the house, stacked the entire porch leading to the front door of the house with a very neat wall of timber.

When they built it up as far as the porch roof they hammered the final blocks into the gap so hard it made the structure completely rigid and compact. It consequently made it impossible to remove any of the blocks from the door entrance by hand.

Can you just imagine, at six o'clock the following morning my colleague coming home, tired and weary, with door key in hand and looking forward to getting to bed, only to be faced with this situation. No slumber because of the lumber!

PORNO SHOP

A new adult shop opened in the City and immediately advertised in the local media that it was selling XXX-rated pornographic videos/dvds and magazines. A self-righteous member of the public made a telephone complaint to a high ranking Garda officer and I was tasked with investigating.

I obtained a search warrant and gathered a large number of Gardaí to brief them about the raid and to assign various tasks to members such as bagging and documenting evidence and exhibits. I cautioned them to behave professionally while in the premises and not to be 'play acting' with any of the plastic or rubber devices or dolls they might encounter! Nothing was to go missing either, I told them!

I was explaining that I did not know the exact layout of the premises and shelving of stock when Garda Reilly immediately intervened and assisted my briefing by declaring,

60

"All the videos are in two aisles of shelving in the middle of the shop and the magazines are along the walls. The plastic goods are on high shelving!"

Immediately the room erupted into laughter and whistles. There were shouts from the back of the parade room,

"How do you know that Reilly? You must be going in there as a customer!"

Reilly was red-faced and attempted to redeem himself and regain his composure as he knew he had just given his colleagues some material to slag him off for months. He protested his innocence by saying,

"No, no. You see, I saw it from looking in the window from the street outside while on foot patrol."

I immediately corrected Garda Reilly before the gathering by saying that this was not possible as there were thick glitzy gold curtains in the window preventing a view inside from the street. Garda Reilly's reply was to make things even worse for himself.

"No, no," he explained. "You can see inside the premises from the street if you get down on you knees and look up the way, under the curtains."

DUMMY IN LETTERKENNY

There was a Garda in Letterkenny who made a false arrest one time. In the course of a violent struggle with a suspected burglar, who resisted arrest, some of the prisoner's limbs were horrifically dismembered from his body. So anxious was this particular Garda to make this prized arrest, ahead of his 'more knowledgeable' colleagues, he enthusiastically rushed the suspect outside a rural shop at Illistrin, Kilmacrennan and grabbed him before he got away.

It transpired that the suspect was actually a plastic mannequin! It was hanging outside the shop and used to display waterproof clothing for sale. Someone had obviously forgotten to take it in when closing the shop for the night.

The story, with the photo, was covered in an internal Garda Representative Association's magazine but was read and taken up by a national radio station. A researcher for Joe Duffy's Liveline show on RTE Radio1 contacted the Garda Press Office, requesting to interview me about the story.

A senior officer from Garda Headquarters contacted me and firmly advised me not to give a radio interview, as,

"Duffy might bend the story in some negative way against the force."

Well Joe, I am now retired and free from the constraints of my former employer! Please feel free to ring me about this incident, anytime!

SCAMMED MILK

Early on in my career I worked in a radio/telephone control room which was also an incident room when anything serious happened along the border in the Donegal Policing Division. At night there were no relief breaks and the entire shift had to be completed, working alone, without leaving the room. You could take a quick dash to the toilet nearby. It was possible sometimes in the middle of the night to take a quick visit downstairs to talk briefly with colleagues on operational duties. However, as soon as the phone rang or the radio crackled, it was a race back to respond.

One night while on duty in the control room I realised I had no milk to make a cup of tea. I went downstairs and spoke to the Sergeant on duty. He had a container of milk and I asked if I could have a 'drop.' He was immediately defensive and refused, unapologetically. The milk was for bringing home for his breakfast, he protested, without any sympathy for my plight. Needless to say I was disappointed and somewhat peeved. When the Sergeant went back out on duty, I came up with a plan. In the medical room where drunken drivers were taken to provide urine or blood samples there were sealed boxes for the doctor to use in extracting samples from them. The blood kit included a sealed, single use, sterilised syringe!

I broke open one of the unused boxes, removed the syringe and went to the Sergeant's milk in the kitchen fridge. Puncturing a hole with the needle on the syringe on the top of the carton I sucked out some of the milk for my tea. Then I thought that the carton would appear too light, so I decided I would need to use the syringe to squeeze water back into the carton. Not one of my proudest moments, but in my wish for retaliation on the Sergeant, I decided to drain out ALL of the milk and replace it completely with water.

Can you imagine the look on the face of the Sergeant the following morning at the breakfast table? Fat-free milk, or should I say, milk-free milk!

TROUBLE DOWN THE LINE

A busy and already harassed Guard answered the phone one day with the simple greeting to the caller,

"Letterkenny here!" The caller's reply was in the tone of controlled anger.

"What do you mean, Letterkenny?"

He went on to rant even further.

"That phone response you gave me could be for Letterkenny Hospital, Letterkenny Social Welfare, Letterkenny Fire Station or wherever. How am I supposed to know who I got through to?"

"Well you rang me. Who did you want to call and anyway who are you?" the Garda replied in a sarcastic tone.

"I wanted Letterkenny Garda Station and for your information I am Garda Assistant Commissioner John Malarkey ... and you are?" he thundered.

The Garda momentarily froze to the spot, his voice fell silent as he saw the end of his career coming at him like a train down a track. He quickly recovered his composure.

"I am the manager, John Maher, and for your information you are through to Letterkenny ... Hospital."

The Officer's tone immediately changed as embarrassment and a feeling of foolishness descended upon him. His hitherto arrogant stance was now subdued.

"Eh ... my apologies. Obviously wrong number," he sheepishly replied before quickly hanging up.

The officer swiftly re-checked the phone number for Letterkenny Garda Station and rang it. The same Garda answered the phone in an extremely polite, slightly altered professional tone and accent,

"Good afternoon, you are through to Letterkenny Garda Station, Garda Purcell here. How can we be of assistance to you?"

"Good man, the Hospital there could learn a thing or two from us about professional phone manners," the officer replied proudly.

SICKO ESCORT AND A ROSE OF TRALEE

When a Guard is off sick, he or she is still subject to compliance with all internal regulations. One such regulation is that the member is prohibited, at pain of disciplinary action, from engaging in any physical activity which could prolong or exacerbate the illness, like someone with back pain doing weight-lifting!

Over the years, quite a few young eligible Gardaí have been successfully recruited or head-hunted to be escorts for competitors in the famous Rose of Tralee Festival. The lucky escorts accompany the young ladies to various social events and meals throughout the festival week. It is a job any single man would die for, considering the line up of beautiful and talented women who successfully get to the final stage of the competition.

One year a particular Rose was being interviewed on stage in Tralee by the host Gay Byrne, when he asked how the girl was getting on with her escort. The Rose went on at great length to explain that her escort was gorgeous and a perfect gentleman. Gay asked the girl to point out her escort down in the crowd, which she did. The cameras covering the event immediately panned in for a close-up in the crowd where a clearly embarrassed individual was seated. His face was beamed across the country and beyond.

The escort had good reason to be embarrassed. He was a young Garda on sick leave! He knew immediately, as he buried his face into his hands, that his bosses were, no doubt, watching him on television. I feel sure his activities at the event did not prolong his illness! In any event, he was not disciplined as it obviously could not be proven, not even by his jealous superiors, that being an escort was a prohibited activity, whether or not on sick leave!

CHAPTER FOUR

LAUGHTER AT THE EXPENSE OF THE PUBLIC WE SERVE

A colleague once said to me,
"This would be a great job, if we did not have to deal with the public."
Of course this was dry wit and humour,
police work is all about dealing with the public.
That said, sometimes the public can be very challenging to handle.
It is no wonder so, that from time to time,
some police officers *play cat and mouse* with the public
when the opportunity arises.

DEAD MAN TALKING!

One day at work I was walking past a colleague's office desk while he was seated there and engaged in a phone conversation. I just managed to hear him say to the person on the other end,

"I regret to inform you mam, Garda Powell died about two weeks ago. Thank you, good bye!"

"Bloody hell," I said to Garda Powell, when he came off the phone, *"why on earth did you tell that person that you were dead?"*

Garda Powell sat back on his chair and started to talk. A few months earlier when he was working nights a lady rang the station from America trying to identify and locate the address of a man she had an encounter with back home. She went on to confide to the by now very curious Garda Powell that she had an affair with this married man who had later returned to Ireland. She wanted to make 'further contact' with him! The lady had only part of an address and a first name.

70

Garda Powell's curiosity was heightened and he himself wanted to identify this interesting Waterford man. Maybe he knew him personally, he thought. Garda Powell asked various questions about the man such as description, address, name used and other details.

However, the lady had only patchy details, if in fact they were truthfully given by the two-timing individual who had charmed her. The American lady was so impressed with the help she was getting from Garda Powell she undertook to get back to him again on a further date with additional details to assist in identifying this mysterious Casanova.

Garda Powell said his interest in the case somewhat faded after that. He went on to tell me that over the months following that first phone call, it became a problem. The lady would regularly ring the station, leave messages, send letters and fax messages addressed to him.

It was getting too much for Garda Powell and he came up with one sure way of terminating contact with this lady. He terminated himself!

ADEQUATE GARDA RESOURCES

Regularly, some of Garda management follow 'the company line,' or should I say, the government line and go before the media protesting that they have adequate resources to serve the public. The reality is that Gardaí on the streets have the complete opposite view and the experience to back it up.

One time at a community meeting in a city station a concerned member of the public asked a Garda Officer how many Gardaí were actually available to police the city at any given time.

Without needing to take a pause, the officer replied with confidence,

"There are twelve patrol cars available in the city, twenty-four hours a day."

The person who posed the question was satisfied, if not impressed with this reply. The reality was that there were twelve patrol cars attached to the station - Traffic, Crime, Uniform, Drugs and the rest, but at any given time a fraction would be operational with actual Gardaí using them on patrol. The rest would certainly be available - parked at the station with not enough resources to drive them!

I guess that during his training that officer missed the lecture where everyone else had to learn off the words,

"The truth, the whole truth, and nothing but the truth."

MIRROR, MIRROR ON THE WALL, WHO IS THE PRETTIEST OF THEM ALL?

A rather portly Garda was on foot patrol down the city centre one night. His ill-fitting stiff uniform shirt tail came out of his trousers while he was walking and swinging his arms. He happened upon a business frontage that conveniently had mirrored glass windows.

Looking around to ensure that it was quiet and no one was about, he pulled up his uniform in front of the convenient 'vanity' mirrored glass. Then he undid his trouser belt, unzipped and partly dropped his trousers before tucking his shirt inside his trousers.

Having completed the task he pulled himself together, leaned forward and admired himself before walking away.

He did not realise that the premises he dressed before was in fact a busy restaurant. It had mirrored one-way glass for the privacy of diners within, seated at the highly sought after window seating. The customers had a ring-side view of the Garda makeover.

That story reminds me of another similar incident.

A colleague and I were in a surveillance van outside the post office many years ago. We were waiting for a drug dealer to collect a postal package containing drugs which had been intercepted in a sorting office.

For obvious reasons, the van we were seated in had the rear window fitted with one-way mirrored glass.

We were approached by this woman who came up to the back of the van. It was perversely weird, two men sitting within a couple of inches of a woman's face, while unknown to her, you saw how she put on her make-up.

She consoled herself as she rubbed away her eye wrinkles, applied lipstick and sorted her hair. She was even talking to herself!

Most women consider their time before a mirror to be an extremely private moment. I am sure this lady would have been mortified if she had known how lacking in privacy her powdering actually was.

KEEP A LOOK-OUT
FOR A RED-FACED, RED-DRESSED WOMAN

There was a busy hotel right along the border behind the old Customs post which had long since closed down. The structure of the Customs post is still there to this day in a state of derelect disrepair.

One night, while on border patrol, a colleague and I drove around the rear of the hotel. We noticed that there was a big function going on inside as we could hear the thud of music and see the silhouetted shapes of people dancing on the other side of the net curtains.

Suddenly, our radio came alive with a message from our base station. We quickly realised that each time I pressed the car radio handset to reply, it caused immediate interference to the music speakers inside the hotel window. The hotel speakers would all but shut down with the feedback from my activation of the car radio.

My disruptive, juvenile, immature nature came up with an idea. I pressed the radio handset and started saying on the radio with a slow perverse tone of voice,

"Wow, take a look at that voluptuous woman down there in the low-cut red dress! I bet she is willing!"

It blared out louder than the music coming from the speakers!

We sped off and left the crowd inside looking around, no doubt in curiosity, at any woman in a red dress. We also left a DJ up on the stage, red faced, trying to gesture embarrassingly to the crowd in front of him that what was just said did not come from his mouth and had nothing to do with him!

PAINTING THE TOWN 'RED'

"Report of suspicious incident at Canada Street. Pool of blood on the pavement and appears to be sourced from an apartment building above location."

"Roger, got that," we replied on our car radio to the station radio control room.

On our arrival at the location we could see a massive pool of what appeared to be human blood on the street pavement. Shining my flash lamp up along the apartment block from the pool of blood, I could see that it was dripping in a stream line down the wall from a specific apartment window ledge above us.

Suspecting something very sinister to have occurred, we raced into the apartment block and went to the door from which the pool of blood came from. We knocked hard on the relevant apartment door and identified ourselves loudly, but after a considerable period of time there was still no reply.

There was nothing for it and without a second thought I stood back from the door, ran at it and kicked it in! The inside was in darkness. We entered a bedroom with a shaft of light coming in through the window. There were two very pale human bodies, a man and a woman, entangled around each other in a grotesque position. Legs and arms were dangling in all directions. We saw blood everywhere, on the window glass, window ledge and on the bed sheets. The lady's face was caked in dry blood. A murder scene was before us, we concluded!

Suddenly, one of the bodies, the lady, moved. She lifted her head and uttered in a drunken, slurred voice,

"What the hell are you perverts doing in here? Get to f*** out!"

Without the slightest embarrassment, both 'bodies' then became fully alive, gathered themselves up and covered their nakedness.

When things settled, the lady told us in a very matter of fact way that in the course of a sexual frenzy she had developed a massive nose bleed. She hung her head out the window for ages, letting the blood flow until it had stopped, before returning to bed and no doubt, the activity which had been so interrupted.

We swiftly left through the smashed door a short time later. When the Radio Control Room contacted us for a status report, I simply replied,

"No further action needed here. At least not from us!"

CASTAWAY

In my time on the beat in a major city there were three or four night club/late bars in close proximity to each other. This made for easier policing with stretched resources, as it contained the crowds to a small enough area for us to monitor.

The difficulty, on the other hand, was that all the revellers from the various establishments spilled out onto the street pavements and roadway at the same time in the early morning. It made it almost impossible for traffic to drive through. Even the police 'Paddy Wagon' could only go through the crowd at a snail's pace as indifferent, drunken, drugged-up individuals, or those who had utter contempt for the law, would very reluctantly move out of the patrol van's path. It was similar to driving through a large flock of sheep or herd of cattle.

On one of these normal weekend nights we came on a disturbance on the street, with two guys beating the lard out of each other. We got out of the van and pulled them apart. The guy I grappled with had a nose and head injury and was bleeding like a defeated boxer having gone twelve rounds! His face, hands, shirt and trousers were covered in his own blood.

I spread him over the bonnet of the 'Paddy Wagon,' searched and cuffed him, before dumping him into the cage in the rear of the van along with his 'companion.' We could hear people within the crowds shouting obscenities at us as we left the scene - 'Pigs,' 'Garda brutality' and the like. A beer bottle hit the van and, as we moved through the crowd, the sides of the van were thumped with peoples fists in misguided and intoxicated anger.

We 'deposited' the prisoners in the station cells and returned to the streets as quickly as possible. This time as we drove through the crowd it was strangely different from before. We could not fathom it out. The crowds became silent as they caught sight of us. Everyone moved out of our path immediately in an almost respectful manner. No one was shouting abuse at us and the look on everyone's face was somewhere between fearful and respectful. We kept patrolling up and down the street without difficulty.

It became the quietest night we ever had and no further arrests were required. When the crowds eventually began to disperse we returned to the station for a break and to process the prisoners we had taken in earlier. It was only then that we solved the reason why we had such a compliant crowd on the streets.

I was reminded of the film 'Castaway' starring Tom Hanks, in which he was washed up on an island after the plane he was on ditched into the sea. He had an injury and his bloodied hand transferred an imprint on a football which almost looked like a human face similar to the famous Turin Shroud!

There on the front bonnet of the 'Paddy Wagon' was a perfectly bloodied transfer imprint of my prisoner's face, arms, hands and body. It looked horrific and intimidating. It gave the impression that we had mercilessly crashed into a pedestrian who got in our way!

Maybe I should have suggested to the authorities that all patrol cars should have this feature stencilled on them as a 'public disorder prevention initiative.' It was with great reluctance that I later washed that blood from the front of that patrol van.

CRANK CALLER

For a time, one of the national radio stations ran an early morning competition for its listeners. It was called 'Car of the Day' and involved announcing a registration number of a car that belonged to someone somewhere in Ireland. If the car owner, a friend or an observant member of the public spotted the car bearing the announced registration number somewhere in traffic and rang in during the show, there was a cash prize.

Totally contrary to regulation, abuse of my position, data protection and all that, on more than a few occasions I checked out the 'radio announced' registration number on the Garda computer. With the name and address of the owner from the computer record I would ring telephone enquiries and get the phone number listed for the relevant name and address. Anonymously, I would ring the number and tell the often 'sleepy head' owner to immediately ring into the radio station to collect the prize. I never said who was calling!

I would then await the radio presenter announcement.

"Wow! That was quick! Our Car of the Day prize has just been won by ..."

Good deed done for the day!

SUPERIOR INTELLIGENCE

Superior

An irate lady rang the Garda station one night complaining about something or other. At the other end of the line was an equally cranky Garda who was famous for not suffering fools gladly. The conversation became heated as it went on until it sounded like 'locked horns.' Getting nowhere the lady demanded to be transferred to the Garda's superior. The cranky Garda who was obviously not short of self esteem, replied,

"Mam, as far as I am concerned there is no one superior to me in this station, or indeed anywhere else in the world for that matter."

Thus ended the lesson and telephone conversation!

Intelligence

A Garda went to a big manor type home on a large country estate one day in response to a report of a burglary. In the course of the Garda's investigation in the mansion there was also a very polite general conversation between him and the owner of the property, who was a retired high ranking British Army officer. The subject of the 'Troubles' in Northern Ireland was mentioned as it featured strongly in the news at the time. The General enquired of the Garda,

"My good man, do you have any serious intelligence in An Garda Síochána?"

The Garda replied proudly,

"Cannot really say overall sir, but I have my Leaving Certificate anyway."

OPPORTUNITY KNOCKED

I knew an old school Garda who was as cute as they come and saw opportunity all around him. He certainly fitted the description, 'It's the hungry eye sees far.'

One night during a bad weather storm a member of the public rang the station and asked to speak to the said old school Guard whom he knew personally. A tree had been knocked down in the storm and was blocking the road to the local GAA sports field. The caller knew that the cute Garda was involved in the local GAA and would want to take a personal interest in sorting out the problem.

The hungry-eyed Guard took the call, noted the details and considered what he was being told by the caller.

"Ring Mickie Joyce," he said, *"he has the gear to cut the tree and tell him I said he was to do it immediately."*

The conversation ended with the bewildered caller agreeing to take on the unexpected added responsibility tasked to him by the wise old owl.

Almost as soon as he hung up the phone the cute old Guard thought of something else and rang back the man he had been speaking to about the knocked tree.

"By the way, when you contact Mickie Joyce tell him to cut that tree into small fire-sized blocks and stack them neatly in the ditch for me to collect tomorrow!"

One man's misfortune is another's opportunity!

IT WAS A CHARITY

This guy came into the public office of the station one day and marched purposefully up to the public counter. He had a large bag in his hand which he smacked down on the counter. It immediately struck me that this man's demeanour was somewhat confrontational, negative and yet smug and arrogant.

True enough, my first impression was to prove correct as he outlined that he had a motoring offence fine to pay and that he was legally entitled to pay it in full with small change! His fine was for £180 punts at the time. He spilled the contents of the bag on the counter with a sarcastic smile beaming from his face. The entire bundle of coins that came from the bag were made up of brass penny coins.

The man folded his arms and had a satisfied expression on his face. He was ready for an argument.

"Ok, you will not get a receipt for your payment until I count the change to ensure the full £180 punts is there," I said.

His facial expression said that he had not bargained for this scenario. I began counting the change, but within a minute or so the phone rang, which took me away from the task in hand for a short while. When I returned to the counter after that call was dealt with, I recommenced counting the coins, one penny, two pennies, three pennies ... from the beginning. The customer was not impressed, but kept it together as if he did not care.

Half-way through the counting another member of the public came in to the station, so I pushed all the coins out of the way of the hatch and indicated that I would deal with that person. I did not want to delay this person with what I was doing.

I signed a passport form for that person who then left satisfied. I used my arm to slide all the coins back into the counter hatch opening to commence counting in front of the owner of the coins. From the beginning, once again, I counted out loudly... one penny, two pennies, three pennies... The fine payer was visibly angry and was just about containing his anger when the phone began ringing again.

"Don't answer that, for f*** sake, take this first instead!" the chap roared.

He pulled cash notes from his wallet, threw them on the counter and then scooped the coins back into the bag he had brought them in. Some of the coins spilled all over the floor in the public area but his pride would not permit him to bend down and pick them up. I quickly counted the £180 punts from the notes, took it and made out a hasty official receipt. He grabbed the receipt in his fist and squashed it into his pocket as he turned to storm out of the station!

"What am I to do with your coins on the floor?" I shouted ever so politely.

"Put them in the charity box," he shouted banging the door behind him.

Whatever about putting the coinage into the charity box, that fellow was certainly 'put in his box'!

CHAPTER 5
THE CUSTOMER GETS ONE UP ON THE POLICE

Most people love to see police officers make a mistake
or a fool of themselves.
It is only natural, when you have an authorative figure
normally holding the high moral ground,
to enjoy when they mess things up.
Today, with video on camera phones and YouTube,
there is ample opportunity to capture the police officer
when he/she falls from grace.

THE ORGY

What was it about people and the horror they had about being caught in pubs after hours by the Guards? It's not so much nowadays, as very few have any fear of authority. It would be nothing more than an amusing story to tell friends that one was caught or fined for such a minor offence. Back in the day however, drinkers would go to extraordinary lengths to escape the dreaded raid.

Over the years, I witnessed grown adults running out doors as if their lives were in immediate risk or they were avoiding the electric chair! Daring escapes out through small toilet windows and rear exits, or hiding behind beer kegs and crates were also the norm. People from all walks of life were reduced to looking like frightened children playing hide-and-go-seek! Even very prominent businessmen, politicians, members of the legal profession and yes, off-duty Gardaí were reduced to this.

The star prize for the most unusual and hilarious escape idea that I ever came across goes to a pub and its customers in a village in Kilkenny. The pub itself was found to be empty, cleared of all customers when

I was admitted by the publican. Not being satisfied, I went upstairs to the living quarters. I could hear all sorts of noise coming from one particular room. There was whispering and giggling going on.

I went into the room to investigate further and found no less than eight people in a double bed trying to hide under a single duvet. There were arms hanging out here, legs hanging out there and rear ends at either end, as it were! They were all fully clothed and protested that they were all staying upstairs as 'friends' of the publican.

This crew may also have been breaking some religious laws, as well as the criminal law!

SMALL NEED FOR SMALLS

During the troubles in the North and along the border many people who lived in the middle of it all became completely acclimatised to security measures. When you would stop a car at a checkpoint, the driver would almost instinctively get out and open the boot and hand over identification.

A body search was almost expected as the norm, particularly by young Northern Ireland men stopped by the then RUC or British Army. They would regularly spreadeagle and assume the search position before even being asked when stopped at a security checkpoint or by a mobile patrol from either side of the border.

We were conducting a checkpoint along the border one weekend night, specifically searching motorists and occupants of buses for drug possession and dealing. That time, hundreds of buses and cars crossed into the south from the north on weekend nights. The occupants went to clubs, dances and discos. We were aware that a lot of drugs came out with some of the revellers. We had access to an old Customs hut beside the checkpoint and anyone who appeared suspect was taken there to be properly searched in private.

I brought this particularly memorable young Derry man into the hut for a search. When I brought him into a room I looked around behind me and before I even spoke to him, he had his pants down around his ankles and placed his hands against the wall in readiness for the search. Astonished at such willing compliance, but even more curious as to why the young man had no underwear on I just had to ask,

"Why are you not wearing any smalls?"

Without any need to think about a considered reply and without any embarrassment, he quickly replied,

"I am hoping to get lucky with a woman tonight and the less that gets in the way, the better!" said the guy, neither into smalls nor small talk!

KEY TO THE CASE

Some Gardaí deal with motoring offences by simply issuing the motorist with a ticket and a few words of advice. Other Gardaí like to drag the pain on by adding an unwelcome law lecture to the already mortified and unfortunate person on the road. Then there are the rare ones, who take pleasure in the hunt, the detection, obvious panic, embarrassment, apologetic and meek demeanour of their victims.

Garda Jim was one of those. He loved detections so much, he could hardly keep the smug smile off his face as he approached his 'captured' motorist. Speeding, illegal parking, lighting or other motoring offences all attracted Garda Jim!

One day while on town foot patrol, he came on a parked, unattended car with its engine running on the main street. The usual orgasmic smile came to his face! He swiftly pulled the keys from the ignition, locked the doors and withdrew to the cover of a nearby shop door entrance. He was hiding and awaiting the arrival of his 'prey.' Within a few minutes the shopkeeper came out to the Guard and enquired if there was a problem.

Garda Jim, in a mischievous and gloating way, shared details of his big case with the shopkeeper and triumphantly told him,

"Watch what happens next!"

This shopkeeper was about to get a unique insight into how Garda Jim operated and how he enjoyed the hunt, detection and torture of his culprit, or should I say, victim.

After a few tense minutes of waiting, the victim, a well-dressed middle-aged woman, approached the car. Garda Jim and the shopkeeper could see the struggle she was having with the locked door. They could clearly see her expression of confusion at first, followed by the horror of the realisation of her dilemma which was written all over her face. Garda Jim knew this was now the time to pounce on his prey and start the lecture and humiliation, to finish off the kill.

"Watch this," he said triumphantly to the shopkeeper, as he walked slowly towards the distraught lady in a manner of authority and confidence.

Garda Jim had just about reached the crime scene and could see the lady was by now frantically searching through her handbag for the lost keys. Suddenly, her facial expression changed from torment and stress to major relief. Out from her bag came another spare set of keys! She opened the car, got in and drove away totally oblivious to the trap she had just escaped from. She left Garda Jim frozen to the spot, jaw dropped with no detection, keys in his hands, not knowing what to do with them and a shopkeeper in stitches of laughter!

SANTA IS SPIRITED AWAY

The first week into the job I was on duty Christmas Day. A senior colleague rushed me to a patrol car as he had a mission on.

He was a staunch non-drinker and proudly wore his Pioneer pin on his uniform breast pocket. Enroute, he explained that he knew a particular pub was illegally open and he hated people being out drunk when they should be at home with their families on Christmas Day.

We arrived at this pub and got in through a rear door. Sure enough, there were five or six men drinking at the bar. There was an uncomfortable silence all round as my officious colleague lectured the customers while taking out his official notebook to take names and addresses.

"What is your name and address, sir"? my colleague said to the first man.

"Santa Clause from Lapland," came the drunken, slurred reply.

Everyone, including myself, started to laugh uncontrollably. Well almost everyone! My colleague went red in the face with rage and his response came quickly and immediately restored the atmosphere to its previous awkwardness and silence.

"Well Santa ... from Lapland ... you are my prisoner," my colleague said loudly.

Santa was marched out of the pub and put into the patrol car. As my colleague drove the prisoner down the road towards the station, Santa said from the back of the car,

"I am sorry about that Mick." He obviously knew my colleague.

"You had to be the smart arse in front of your friends, didn't you, John?" my colleague replied angrily.

Before I knew it we had passed the station and arrived at a house a few miles outside of town.

"Right, out you get Santa, and behave yourself in future," said my colleague as the humble man got out of the car and walked towards his own front door, Lapland!

CHAPTER 6
GETTING THE BETTER
OF THE CRIMINALS AND PRISONERS

There is sheer frustration in dealing with criminals who,
most of the time, appear to have the laws on their side.
So, it is obvious that if a police officer gets an opportunity
to have a laugh and one up on a criminal,
he or she will grab the chance!

HOT PURSUIT

There was this criminal who was 'a walking crime wave' throughout the county. Burglaries, robberies and reckless car chases with Gardaí were the norm when he was at large. The crime statistics were going through the roof in the Division, almost totally attributable to this one individual. He was nearly intercepted a couple of times but always managed to make a daring escape across the border. He took major risks for himself and anyone who got in his way.

He was finally arrested in the course of one of his crime rampages, but managed to escape from the Garda custody interview room when left unsupervised for a few minutes.

Embarrassed Gardaí vowed that if and when he was captured again, he would not escape.

Eventually, he literally 'ran out of road' one night in a car chase with Gardaí. He had written off his car, or should I say, someone else's car, in a roadside ditch that refused to get out of his way. He was arrested, once again. This time he was broken up, injured and in pain, so he was taken immediately to the local hospital for treatment. Although now a prisoner, he was admitted to hospital.

A Garda was posted outside his bedroom round the clock to keep an eye on him. That member was well aware and fully briefed about his track record. The Garda on protection duty vowed that this infamous prisoner would not embarrass him by escaping 'on his watch.' He decided the solution was to handcuff the prisoner to his bed or a radiator in the room to ensure that no spectacular escape would take place in the dead of night. The Garda did this without any regard to the objections and protests of the prisoner.

Later, while half asleep in the corridor of the hospital outside the prisoner's bedroom, the Garda was alerted to this almighty screaming coming from the prisoner's room. He rushed in and found him wriggling about in the bed in agony. He appeared to be having a heart attack or some sort of seizure. The monitors for blood pressure, heart rate and what-not were bleeping away loudly. The night nurses were quick on the scene.

It turned out that in the middle of the night, the painkiller medication the prisoner was on obviously wore off. Also, the handcuffs were attached to the bedside radiator which had come on during the night and became extremely hot.

It did not take long for the heat to be conducted through the metal handcuffs before zapping the prisoner in his sleep!

Was this a form of justice or injustice? You decide!

NAKED ANGER

Drunken prisoners in cells are normally very noisy and disruptive. They keep banging on the steel cell door and roar all types of abuse which echoes throughout the station because the acoustics in the large cell accentuates the noise pitch. One night, a colleague of mine was really frustrated with the noise and torrents of abuse coming from a drunk in the cell. In barely controlled anger he said to me,

"I would love to go down to that cell and kick the s*** out of that f***er."

I replied sympathetically that I felt his pain but explained that it would not be worth losing his job over such a dramatic illegal act. The reply my colleague gave was so immediate and obviously thought out I did not know if he meant it or not.

"No, no," said he, *"I know a foolproof way to sort him out without ever getting into trouble!"*

Curiosity got the better of me of course and I asked how that could be done with such impunity.

"If we stripped down completely naked and went into the cell and beat the crap out of him, we would never get in trouble for it!" he replied immediately.

"Why would you not get in trouble for that?" I said, totally perplexed and somewhat disturbed by the notion.

"Come on, what Internal Affairs investigators would believe a drunk complaining that two big naked Gardaí came into his cell and beat the crap out of him!" he said with complete confidence.

IRISH INVASION OF RUSSIAN TERRITORY

Historically, it is well documented that Napoleon Bonaparte's French troops and later, Hitler's German army, made unsuccessful attempts to occupy Russia. Up until now, there has been no such historic record of the small group of Irish people who, in more recent years, invaded, and might I add, successfully occupied Russia.

A few years ago, when stationed in Waterford City I dealt with a group of people who travelled round the country making a career out of 'invading property.' The group normally consisted of four or five large families with vans and caravans. They would take over Church or hotel car parks at the beginning of a busy bank holiday weekend. Within minutes, discussions with the local clergy or hotel management would take place and they would move on swiftly, having been compensated for the inconvenience of vacating the property.

One particular bank holiday weekend, they moved from various places between Dublin and Wexford, and stopping along the way, were compensated by no less than three churches and two hotels to help with 'resettlement.' Hotel managers panicked that the presence of caravans and vans in the car parks might affect business and deemed it more prudent to 'make a settlement.'

Hoteliers began ringing each other to warn of the possible arrival of the group to other businesses.

Finally, the group arrived in Waterford and took up residence in the car park in front of a luxury hotel outside the city. As usual, management of the hotel confronted the group and requested that they move on. A representative of the group made it clear that they had no where else to go and could only go into a caravan site it they had €1,000. The hotel manager enquired if €100 would suffice.

"No," was the resounding answer. "The cost is €1,000... per caravan!" he added.

The representative also intimated that more caravans were on the way, with lots of children anxious to go to the toilet. However, he did have some good news! If the situation could be 'sorted' with them, they would ensure that not only would they immediately move on, but also the other caravans yet to arrive would not be coming.

This time, however, the initiative did not work! In fact, it completely backfired. The hotel owners refused to pay and a stand-off ensued. Very early the following morning a large number of farmers with tractors and trailers arrived into the hotel car park. They parked their trailers in a corral around the caravans and vans. The 'visitors' were now boxed in and could not move out even if they wished. The high ground for negotiation had, as it were, shifted. A mini-riot ensued between hotel security staff and the group of unwanted visitors. We were called and a riot van full of Gardaí, including myself, rushed to the scene.

Upon arrival, we were faced with utter chaos. I was the senior member in charge of the Gardaí present. Fights and arguments were breaking out all round us and allegations of damage to vans and tractors were being reported to us, or should I say, screamed at us. There was even a lady lying on the ground claiming that the hotel tractor had run over her legs. She demanded an ambulance even though she sometimes managed to get up off the ground to confront Gardaí who attempted to arrest her relatives. When she heard the sound of the ambulance siren getting nearer, she hit the ground immediately and continued with her moaning. It was beyond farcical. (I learned later that she was released from hospital within minutes of being examined by a doctor, as no injuries were found!)

Arrests were made, and at the Garda station, I negotiated with the group. It was agreed that they would be charged with various public order offences to appear in court on a later date and immediately released, on condition that they undertook to collect their caravans, vehicles and family members, and leave the area immediately. Peace was restored and the agreement honoured. My pride in helping to defuse the situation would be short lived!

The following evening while relaxing at home, off duty, watching the evening news, I nearly choked on my dinner, when, to my utter shock, one of the top stories featured a group of travellers who had occupied the grounds of the Russian embassy in Dublin. There was a standoff with Gardaí who had no jurisdiction to go into the Russian property and deal with the 'invaders.' The Russian security staff also appeared to be helpless as how best to deal with the situation. Interviewed on the news was one of my 'visitors' from the day before in Waterford. It was the same group. The spokesperson for the group told the interviewer that they had nowhere else to go and the situation could be resolved with a "little initiative" by the Russian embassy or Irish authorities.

I laughed aloud at the sheer neck and innovation of this enterprising group and thanked the stars that it was not me trying to sort out this one, considering I would not even be able to set foot on foreign soil. I suspect that they successfully negotiated with the Russians and moved on eventually, with a wad of roubles in their pockets.

CROCODILE DUNDEE GETS BITTEN

While stationed in New Ross, Co Wexford a few years ago I dealt with a dispute at a local hotel. It started with a phone call to the station from a distressed hotel manageress. Customers were refusing to pay an accommodation bill. Along with two other Gardaí, I responded to the call and on arrival was greeted in the foyer with the sight of a very large group of travellers. Some were seated and the rest were standing around all over the place. There must have been more than twenty in the group.

The manageress approached me and explained that one of the group had come to reception on behalf of the rest and said they were only willing to pay for one room. This representative had argued that he had wanted only one room for the group and that it was the hotel's mistake that they had provided over eight rooms.

While speaking to the manageress I noticed out the side of my eye that this particular individual had come over near us and sat down. It was obvious that this man was listening in to our conversation. I gestured to the manageress and she whispered that he was the group spokesman. I suggested to her that we move away to a more private place in the reception area. She agreed, but once again, this man got up from his seat, followed us and stood close to us. In a very animated fashion he began looking around him and at the ceiling, pretending to be oblivious to our presence.

"Excuse me, can we have tea and coffee for everyone here, including the Gardaí," he suddenly called to a passing waitress.

"Absolutely not," the waitress replied, before stomping off.

The crowd began laughing and jeering. I had enough at this point and in an equally animated manner said loudly to the manageress,

"Ask for the bill to be paid in full from the 'spokesman' and if he refuses, I will arrest him and his room partners."

The spokesman retained his smug, confident face while he continued to smirk. Needless to say, when the manageress made the request again, he refused to pay the bill. I arrested him and his wife before marching them through the crowd and out the door to the patrol car. None of the crowd was laughing now. I noticed the confusion on their faces as if a plan was unexpectedly falling apart.

At the station, the spokesman prisoner and his wife argued with a colleague of mine that it was a civil matter between the hotel and customers, and under the law we had no such powers of arrest. I explained that they were correct in their interpretation of the law as it was up until recently. He still had his smug, confident look and his arms were folded as if to shield or disregard what I was saying. I explained further that very new legislation had recently been put in place and there was a power of arrest because their action was categorised as a crime rather than a debt. I could see him make insecure looks in the direction of his wife from time to time but he did not flinch.

Suddenly, I started to laugh aloud and said to him,

"Did anyone ever tell you that you are the spitting image of your man in the Crocodile Dundee film?"

Everyone, including his wife, began to laugh in agreement with me, except Crocodile Dundee himself! His face suddenly changed from being arrogant and confidant to pale and insecure.

"I want a solicitor," he said.

I had him on the run! I presented him with a list of local solicitors and as he selected one, he kept saying to me in a sarcastic tone,

"You're a funny lad. You're a very funny lad."

When the solicitor arrived, the prisoners were briefed in private for a few minutes. The next time I saw the prisoners their facial expressions had completely changed. The confident smug arrogance that radiated from them up to this point was now gone. It was replaced by faces of resignation and failure.

Crocodile Dundee shouted over to his wife,

"Go on, pay them."

She complied by sticking one of her hands down her ample breast cleavage and withdrew a very large wad of cash notes which were tightly rolled up. The money was handed over to me and I counted out the full cost of the hotel accommodation bill before returning the rest to the lady.

The case was closed at this point and the prisoners released. I guess on this occasion Crocodile Dundee and his wife got well and truly bitten in the pocket, or more correctly, the breast pocket!

BIKERS - BACK TO THE FUTURE

After An Garda Síochána's inception back in 1922, the bicycle was the main mode of transport for most Gardaí on patrol, particularly in rural areas. In later years, when bikes were all but replaced by patrol cars, members were still required to own and maintain a bike. From time to time in the 1960s and 70s officers on station inspections would require the Gardaí to present the bikes for inspection. This was more about ensuring that the Gardaí did not get an allowance for buying and maintaining a bike unless they actually had one. It was a formality. In the 1980s and 90s, Gardaí did not use bikes.

In 2000, I started using my mountain bike to patrol Waterford city at night. I believed it was a quick, silent and efficient way of covering the city on patrol. Some of my colleagues were less than impressed from the very start. It was not cool and it was an obvious embarrassment to them. Some would avoid making eye contact as they cruised past me in the patrol cars in the city centre.

On the first night, I was patrolling through an estate of houses and overheard a domestic in progress as I silently cycled past a particular house. I called for backup and after gaining entry to the house I stopped a drunken husband beating his wife. My colleagues gave begrudging credit to the fact that if I had been in a patrol car the domestic fight and shouting would not have been heard.

The second night while cycling the wrong way up a one way street, I met a suspicious looking fella obviously scrutinising a shop front. He did not see me or hear my approach. I could see him looking at the first floor level of the building checking for alarms and cameras. He was totally in shock when I was right up in his face before he had time to think, let alone run for it.

He was wearing rubber gloves and concealing a tyre-lever type jemmy bar and knife under his jacket. I arrested him for possession of suspected house-breaking equipment, and called the patrol car to carry the prisoner and bike back to base.

We also found his car in the alley behind the same shop, ready to carry away the proceeds of a burglary he was about to commit.

Later that same morning, along with colleagues, I searched the prisoner's house and recovered thousands of euro worth of stolen outdoor gear, surf boards, wet suits, and the like, from a previous burglary of a similar premises in another town.

The following night three of my colleagues approached me at work, volunteering to do cycling patrols of the city using bikes recovered and impounded at the station.

I attended the weekly crime review meeting at the station later that same week and tried to sell the advantages of cycling patrols to prevent and detect crime. The Superintendent had horror written all over his face as I spoke. He expressed the hope that I had not been cycling around on a bike in public while in uniform. I knew that was the end of my initiative, and that ended that.

Some years later, a very progressive and forward thinking officer, Commissioner Patrick Byrne, was appointed. He had worked abroad with other police services and had witnessed their use of horses, helicopters and… bicycles! He embraced the concept fully and quickly brought back their use into daily Garda work.

The Garda patrol bicycle had come of age once again and is in use in most cities and large towns throughout the country. Sometimes old ways are best, no matter how much technology the modern world comes up with.

IN TOTAL CONFIDENCE

Today Gardaí have very secure digital radios for communications among members on mobile, foot patrols and base stations. It was not so a number of years ago, when anyone with a half decent Ham/CB radio could listen into Garda radio traffic.

A clear example of this can be illustrated by an experience I had while working in a city centre Garda Station. One night, there was a burglary at a rural pub some distance from the city. When patrol cars approached the scene from different directions, one member with a hunch, said over the radio to me, "That will be the work of the Regan's, no doubt!" Another member got back on the radio and agreed with that hunch. They were referring to an infamous family of criminals who operated out of the city.

Within less than a minute the phone rang at the Garda Station and a very angry member of the said Regan clan of criminals berated the Garda at the end of the phone. The caller said most emphatically that none of their family was involved in that burglary.

"We are all out here at home and you can come out here right now to prove it!"

The only thing proved that night was that we needed more secure radios.

A week later, one of the same clan was caught shoplifting in the city centre and was being processed at the Garda Station. I was Custody Sergeant and needed to get cash bail for the prisoner before releasing him. I picked up the radio handset and said over the airwaves,

"Mary Regan, your son Paddy is in here for shoplifting and will not be released until you drop in €100 bail money. Ok?"

Within two minutes the station phone rang and Mary, the prisoner's mother, was at the other end.

"Ok, I am on my way in," she said, *"but would €50 do as that is all I have on me?"*

Enough said!

ROMANTIC BED AND BREAKFAST

It is not unusual for prisoners in police cells to roar and shout abuse. Some will kick the cell door, write on walls, get sick and go to the toilet all over the place demanding attention to wreak revenge against their captors.

One particular night a prisoner was roaring for attention. The Custody Garda noticed that the screams and pleading of the prisoner for Garda assistance appeared more genuine and heartfelt than usual. When the Garda checked on the prisoner he was crying and pleaded to be put in another cell. His request was granted and while being transferred, the prisoner told the Garda that the other drunken male prisoner in cell number 3 had made a number of 'amorous' approaches, which caused him to freak out.

A short time later, a young man was found breaking into a car along the quays in Waterford by a vigilant Garda patrol car crew that happened on the crime in progress. As the arrest was about to be made, the criminal threw the stolen property from the car into the River Suir.

Back at the station the prisoner was interviewed, and although it was obvious that he was guilty, he refused to admit in writing to the crime. He was a cocky prisoner with loads of street attitude.

After a couple of hours interviewing the prisoner without success, the interviewing Gardaí were despondent and came to update me on the lack of progress. They had enough evidence even though the stolen property was not recovered. A statement of admission would have sealed the case for a prosecution.

"You two take a break, and give the prisoner a break also. Put him in a cell to think about his situation. It might focus him," I said.

The lads put the prisoner in a cell... number 3.

Ten minutes later, the banging started on cell door number 3. It was our friend, a now not so cocky, street-wise prisoner. He was pleading to get out and wanted to make a statement of admission!

No doubt, by showing the love, the amorous approach of the drunken gay guy was better at extracting admissions than the Garda 'good cop, bad cop' method of interview!

BUD LIGHT

Unless it's a late night alarm activation, the early morning tour of duty is the busiest time for business premises burglaries to be reported to Gardaí. Owners and staff arrive for work and discover the break-in from the night before.

On one such morning I was on patrol car duty when I had a radio message, directing me to a reported burglary at Mc Ginley's Bar, Lower Main Street, Letterkenny. On my arrival, a staff member was there and the usual signs of a break-in from a rear fire exit door were visible. Missing from stock were bottles of spirits and crates of bottled Budweiser beer. I took note of the details, including the value of the stock, for my Incident Crime Report.

For some reason, before leaving the scene, I decided to search the back of the premises and adjoining fields in case any of the 'loot' had been stashed there. I thought that youths were involved. This would mean they would not have been able to bring their ill-gotten goods home. Besides, crates of beer are pretty heavy and impossible to conceal, without transport. It was just a hunch.

My hunch was quickly rewarded when I stumbled upon two crates of beer hidden in bushes in a field behind the bar. I wondered what I would do as it could be hours, if not days, before the culprits would return. My boss would not allow me to sit on surveillance of a couple of crates of beer for even an hour!

Conscious of possible fingerprints, I carefully removed the beer crates from the field. In a moment of mischief, I came up with a plan, hoping to have one up on the thieves! I asked the barman to fill two crates of used Budweiser bottles with water, then pressed the caps back on and put the crates of 'special' beer back in the hiding place in the field.

Later in the afternoon, as I was about to finish duty, I told another Guard starting work what I had done and we had a laugh.

That same evening I had a phone call at home from my work colleague. The good news was that the burglars had been caught. He said that they were found down the town extremely drunk, from consuming the stolen bottles of spirits they had already polished off. They were found at the early stages of consuming the contents of dark brown Budweiser bottles, drunkenly oblivious to the fact that they were drinking water!

NEVER THUMB A LIFT FROM STRANGERS

Intruder alarms at business premises are the bane of all operational police officers on patrol. Some shops and factories have alarms that are faulty and go off so regularly. Sometimes, police are almost half-hearted in response to check out these particular premises. Other alarms activate in storms and strong winds or when there has been a power cut. That said, we obviously still respond, but mostly with little expectation of an arrest. In a minority of alarm activations, calls to police actually prove to be a genuine case of an intruder.

At about three o'clock one morning in Letterkenny, while on mobile patrol, we got a radio message, "Alarm activation at the Dry Arch Pub." For a change, we were immediately interested in this activation. It was a busy weekend night, the premises was outside the town in a fairly remote area with few houses nearby. It was not a stormy night and the pub was not a habitual false or faulty alarm activator. The hour of the night was about right and the availability of alcohol, cigarettes and possibly cash made me believe this was a genuine call out. We 'hit the pedal' and went as fast as possible.

We arrived at the scene within two minutes. One of the panels in the front door was kicked in and the internal alarm was still going off loudly. I ran to the door and squeezed myself in through the broken small panel. I suddenly felt vulnerable sticking my head into the darkness with half of my body either side of the door. I flicked on my flash light as I wriggled my way in. Immediately, there was a startled looking face captured in the beam of my flash light. I shouted something but with the ear piercing noise of the alarm I'm sure this young man, with dark black hair and pimpled pale face, did not hear me.

I rushed through the gap and the image had vanished. I swept through each room in the dark and also checked the toilets, but alas, no sign. Then I spotted that the rear emergency exit door was partly open. I was so dejected that the burglar had escaped into the darkness. I ran out the back door and there to my delight was my colleague in the process of detaining three suspects in a red van. Unfortunately, my suspect was not one of them. We took the three prisoners back to the station and had them detained and temporarily placed in cells. We believed that my suspect would be somewhere out there, running through fields and attempting to get to the border to make good his escape. We exchanged our marked uniform patrol car for an unmarked detective car from the motor pool at the station and threw ordinary clothes (civvies) over our uniforms, before returning to the area.

We patrolled out the dual carriageway towards Derry in the hope of catching sight of our wanted man. It was a long shot, we felt. To our complete surprise it was not long before we met a man who jumped out of the roadside ditch before our eyes and thumbed a lift from our car. We stopped and the grateful man jumped into the rear of the car, expressing gratitude for stopping as he settled into the seat. For the second time that same night I again shone my flash light into a person's face, and lo and behold, it turned out to be the same face. With the thrill of the chase and capture, it made me shout out, *"Got ya!"*

We could not believe our luck and it made the night for us. Some time later in court, when the facts of the case were outlined in evidence and the young man convicted, the judge in summation said with a smirk on his face to the audience before him,

"I guess the moral of this case is
– never take lifts from strangers

DUMB CRIMINALS CARRYING DUDS

A petrol station was visited by two criminals in New Ross, and after purchasing petrol and a few other things a forged €50 note was handed over. It was immediately copped as a dud by the sharp-eyed shop assistant. Following a brief confrontation about the matter, the two criminals fled the scene.

A couple of hours later, however, the criminals, on reflection, got cold feet about the transaction, when they considered the real possibility of being identified on CCTV in the garage shop.

The inexperienced criminals tried to defuse the situation by ringing the petrol station. They agreed to go back and pay with a real €50 note. They pleaded their innocence over the phone about not knowing that the note they had tendered was a forgery. They had simply panicked when confronted and that explained their speedy departure. The shop manager agreed to deal with them favourably if they called back in person. We were immediately contacted by him after the telephone conversation ended.

When the criminals arrived at the petrol station I pounced and confronted them for questioning. A search of them and their car obviously proved negative. There were no more notes to be found. They had time to cover themselves, or so they had thought. If they were prosecuted they would most likely get off, as they had only presented one forged note, something that any innocent member of the public could take as part of change in daily shopping. Had they more than one forged note in their possession it would make such a defence of innocence less likely. They made sure they were 'clean' when they went back to the shop.

I was about to give up the search of the car when suddenly a mobile phone on the passenger seat made a signal, indicating a text message had been received. I boldly picked up the phone and read the text message.

"Do you need more notes for your shopping in Waterford tomorrow?"

Bingo! I had them. I texted back.

"Sure thing, meet me at the public park in New Ross in half an hour."

"Ok" was the swift repky. My bluff appeared to have worked.

I drove the two prisoners to the station, lodged them swiftly and along with another colleague, changed into civic clothing. We went to the small public park in New Ross and kept a look out for a likely target. There were a few people there, and after some time, I decided to ring the number to see if someone would pick up and answer a phone in the park at the same time. The trick did not work, and despite sending a number of texts enquiring as to the failure to turn up, the person at the other end did not reply. Suspicion must have been aroused at the other end, I thought.

Back at the station the prisoners were still trying to bluff their way out of things. As a last ditch effort I rang the number on the mobile phone from which the earlier text was sent. I used an unidentified land line to make the call, and it worked! A lady answered the phone. I simply said impatiently,

"Get your arse down here to the Garda station immediately and explain yourself or I will go up there and arrest you."

She sheepishly asked who I was and went on to protest that she did not know what I was on about.

"Look, for the last time, get down here within the hour, or I am going up there to arrest you like your two friends here, who are singing like birds."

I hung up before she had any other probing questions. I had made reference in my conversation with the unidentified individual at the other end of the phone to key words such as *"down here"* and *"up there."* This was because I knew the station was at the bottom of a hill in the town, surrounded by commercial premises. Most of the houses were 'up' from the station and I wanted it to appear that I knew where the lady lived in the town. I knew I could have been wrong. She may not have even been from the area, but I had nothing else to go on.

Not within an hour, but within ten minutes, a woman in a very nervous state arrived at the station. She was initially pleading total ignorance about any dud notes. I got her name and made it known to the other two in the cells that their friend was now also in the station. Their plan crumbled on a pure bluff. They all admitted their involvement and later in a derelict house outside New Ross, I recovered a large bundle of dud notes and cannabis.

Can you imagine after their release from custody, the de-briefing the three would have engaged in to establish who broke first?

ENGINE BACKFIRE

At some stage you must have heard a car engine backfire on a street with the characteristic loud noise, similar to the bang of a shotgun. This happens when the petrol to air mix is too strong in the engine, or so I have been told.

The following story is about a backfire with a 4x4 SUV engine, but nothing to do with petrol and air mixtures being incorrectly set in the engine!

During the Celtic Tiger years in Ireland, one of the signs of financial achievement was to drive around in a big 4x4 SUV 'gas guzzler.' Most of these 'tanks' never saw the countryside, let alone rough terrain.

When the economic boom went south, a lot of these environmentally unfriendly forms of transport were for sale, as their owners struggled with maintenance costs, repayments of hire purchase, road tax and fuel costs. Their value plummeted and it became difficult to sell them on and to downsize.

One such cash strapped 4x4 SUV owner, who was a bit of a rogue, came up with a perfect solution to get rid of his particular financial problem. He decided to set up a hoax traffic accident with his SUV and write it off for a fraudulent insurance claim. The plan was to claim that the 4x4 developed an engine defect while being driven, which would cause it to career off the road and become so badly damaged that it would be deemed a write-off. An insurance claim would follow with a cash settlement to sort out some problems.

The 4x4 was taken to a quiet mountain road and pushed over the side. The brilliant plan immediately unravelled because the SUV only rolled down the steep cliff edge a short distance and became embedded in a large boulder. Other traffic happened to come on the scene and stopped. A well-meaning motorist 'assisted' the rogue owner of the

4x4 by calling a tow truck before he could put his plan back on track. The SUV was recovered in remarkably good condition. The bumper and front underside were damaged. In an attempt to salvage some money from the botched-up crime, the rogue subsequently submitted a claim to his insurance company. The claimant indicated that he was not at fault in the single car accident and that it was an engine failure or brake failure which had caused the jeep to go out of control while he was driving.

This sparked an immediate investigation by the insurance company and the manufacturers. This serious allegation could result in a total recall of all similar models by the manufacturer, if such a defect were to be identified.

The whole plan 'backfired' on the rogue claimant when, sometime later, he got a telephone call from the manufacturers of the 4x4 in Japan. The specialist on the phone was from the engine computer section and went on to tell Mr Rogue that they had carried out a forensic computer diagnostics on his 4x4 engine.

The specialist explained that at the time of the accident, the engine ignition had not been on and no one was even seated in the vehicle as the seat belt alarm had not been activated.

There ended the claim, for one of Irelands dumbest criminals!

DEAR MILKMAN
NO BURGLARS TODAY PLEASE

Before going on holidays with their family a very wise couple asked a retired Garda neighbour to keep an eye on their house while they were away. They had carried out all the crime prevention ideas, such as post collection, arranging for rubbish bins to be left out and cancelling the milk delivery.

True to his word, the retired Garda kept an eye on the home over the following days. One night however, really late, he realised he had forgotten to leave out the neighbour's rubbish bin. When he went to the back of the house to get the bin he noticed the back door was broken and wide open. He rushed into the house and heard noise coming from the sitting room area. The good neighbour opened the sitting room door only to find four young juvenile burglars sitting around on the sofas and chairs. To add insult to injury, they were drinking the spirits that belonged to the owners of the house.

It is not known who was more surprised by the encounter, the burglars or the good neighbour. The ex-Garda composed himself and told them that they were all under arrest and not to move. He shut the door and immediately rang the Gardaí. For a time, the retired Garda was vulnerable on his own in the house with these four young 'hooched up' burglars.

When I arrived along with other Gardaí, the burglars were still sitting there drinking casually and very composed as if they had not a care in the world. It became clear later that the burglars thought that there were loads of Gardaí outside at the time! That explained why they did not do a runner before back-up arrived.

It emerged that one of the burglars was the son of a milk delivery man. Unknown to his hard-working father, the son read the notes left for his father by customers cancelling the milk deliveries while they were on holiday.

A pattern was found in previous undetected burglaries and others were subsequently solved when we compared the milkman's customer details against crime in the area!

RUNAWAY CAR

You have often been in a situation such as a debate or argument with someone where later you regret the way you handled it or said something.

This story is a situation I found myself in, and what I said could not have been more appropriate and timely.

I stopped a known criminal and drug dealer at a checkpoint. When I checked his expensive car I commended him for the very clean windscreen, to which he cynically replied,

"Thank you officer."

He was always composed and full of self-control when stopped by Gardaí. He disguised his contempt for us really well. I became more officious in the tone of my voice as I went on,

"It's clean because it's clear of any tax disc and insurance certification."

The criminal immediately 'blew his gasket' with sheer anger. He obviously had enough of being stopped and checked by so many Gardaí that he finally flipped with me. He quickly jumped out of the car and roared into my face,

"You can have the f***ing car. I can afford more cars than you could dream of on your crap wages!"

"Is that not your car rolling down the hill there?" I said most politely as I put my face up to his.

In his fury and rush to get out of his car, he had forgotten to put on the handbrake!

He looked behind him and his face drained of blood and his mouth dropped before he ran like a lunatic after his car down the hill. Heroically he managed to catch up with the car, open the door while it was still in motion and jumped in before yanking up the hand brake. He brought the car to a dramatic stop before it had collided with anything. I walked down the road towards him and had the pleasure of saying to him most courteously,

"Thanks for saving my car!"

I then seized it from him!

Out of breath from running and shock, he sat there unable to speak, his veneer of arrogance in smithereens.

Not many days at work were as good as that one!

HAVE A HAPPY PRISON-FREE NEW YEAR!

There was this criminal who lived in a very isolated rural area. His house was at the end of a long country road with no other approach possible. It was all but impossible to get to this property by car without being seen for about a mile down the road. He also had a loud barking dog which made approaching the place unannounced from the surrounding fields all the more difficult.

I got a 'whisper' from a confidential source that there was a stolen car out of view at the rear of that particular criminal's house. Considering the terrain I have just described, I wondered for a while how I could confirm this intelligence before I could have enough information to acquire a search warrant.

Eventually, I came up with a plan and at eleven o'clock one specific night I walked most of the way up the dark country road leading to the criminal's house. I ducked into the hedges when a car or two passed my way. I then took to crossing the fields when I came close enough to the house. I kept far enough away so as not to alert the guard dog. Then I waited and waited for the midnight hour. Just before it struck twelve I crawled beneath a hedgerow which was clearly overlooking the rear of the man's house.

Suddenly, all hell broke loose with the noise of crashing glasses, and the roars of laughter and song from within the house. The dog began barking furiously at me as it tried to yank free from its chain. The dog's efforts were completely ignored by the revellers inside as they sang in and rejoiced in the New Year. I swiftly moved closer, got my confirmation on the identification of the stolen car before silently retreating into the night darkness.

That's how sad my life was in ringing in the New Year back in 2006!

CHAPTER 7
COURT CASES AND JUDGES

The Courthouse can be a very formal, if not boring place to work,
most of the time. The majority of police officers hate the hours
sitting in court awaiting their cases to be dealt with
and more often than not, only to learn
that the case is to be adjourned, once again.

Sometimes, unexpected humour occurs in the court
which briefly replaces the formality with a laugh.
There is that fear that if you laugh out loud in court
you could get seven days for contempt.
You are best advised to treat the judiciary like royalty
and only laugh if they laugh.
Remember, never laugh louder than the judge!

STAR WITNESS

I knew a judge once who was particularly friendly with a character of a Garda who worked in a very small rural village on the coast of Ireland. On court day Garda Brannon would regularly meet and greet the judge when he arrived in town for the court sitting. Garda Brannon would carry the judge's bag of files and legal reference books into the private chamber at the rear of the court. Once inside, the door closed and they, in the most informal sense, gossiped and chatted about all sorts of matters. At times, shrieks of laughter would be heard coming from this room where the Garda had a private audience with the judge.

At the same time, the very silent court room would be full of solicitors, Gardaí, witnesses and defendants anxiously awaiting the eventual grand entry of 'My Lord.'

Eventually, the judge would leave the chamber for his court bench and his face would switch quickly to a grey, very formal, professional expression, as did Garda Brannon's.

To the astute observers of body language, it was well-noted that when the judge had made his mind up on a case, he always folded his arms and put his head down. It did not matter what additional formal evidence or proofs were given after this stage as he had made up his mind to convict.

I was present one day when a very boring case involving a traffic accident was before the judge. There was long-winded evidence being given by Gardaí and witnesses. Measurements of the scene and details of positions of crashed cars were being studied on sketch maps and it was still unclear to the judge who was at fault in the accident.

Suddenly, in the Garda evidence a solicitor questioned if he had taken the scene measurements himself to which the Garda replied,

"I was assisted by Garda Brannon who arrived on the scene by chance while off duty."

The judge's face lit up!

"Is Garda Brannon here in the court?" he shouted.

From the crowd at the rear of the packed court Garda Brannon shouted up,

"I am here judge."

Without required rules of evidence, the legal requirement to get into the witness box, being sworn in and giving formal evidence, Garda Brannon was questioned by the judge across the crowded court room.

"Garda Brannon, was it a bad accident, or what?"

Garda Brannon shouted back, forgetting the need for formality and due decorum.

"God, Judge, it sure was, with a rubber skid mark of fifteen feet long burned into the road, he must have been speeding. He is guilty all right!"

The defending solicitor objected and went on at some length, protesting to the judge all sorts of legal points and interpretations of his reading of the accident sketch maps. The solicitor blabbered on, but did not spot the signals.

The judge had just folded his arms and was looking down at his own bench. Decision made!

ONE LAW FOR ONE...

Someone's mobile phone rang loudly in the body of the court in the middle of a case being heard by a judge who had no tolerance for such disrespect.

The judge stopped proceedings and loudly announced to all present,

"The next mobile phone that goes off in my court will lead to the owner being in contempt of court and I will give them a seven-day custodial sentence."

He then resumed hearing the case before him.

Within a minute or two another mobile phone went off! With red-faced embarrassment the owner of the phone struggled with his clothing in a frantic effort to silence the noise as quickly as possible.

It was the judge's personal mobile phone!

A SURE WAY OF SECURING A CONVICTION

There was a judge who was not sympathetic to the relentless drunken abuse Gardaí experienced on the streets at night. He believed, and regularly pontificated from his bench, that Gardaí, unlike other members of the public, were paid to take verbal abuse. It was a misuse of the Public Order Act for Gardaí to prosecute people in such incidents, in his opinion. This infuriated a particular Garda so much that he came up with a sure way of changing the judge's attitude.

A young drunk who was very abusive and threatening with this Garda was arrested and taken to the station to be processed. This involved reading over the charges/offence, followed by a legal caution and then inviting the prisoner to make a reply, known as a response to the charge. The response by the prisoner, if any, is recorded in writing by the member and it may be given in evidence in court. Most prisoners make no reply, or simply say, 'Not guilty.' This particular prisoner responded rather differently to the charge,

"F*** you!"

The Garda looked down shaking his head, pretending to be seriously hurt by the remark, and then said,

"The judge will not be impressed with that reply!"

"And f*** the judge too!"

The Garda eagerly wrote this further reply down and read it out in court in evidence to the judge on a later date. Horrified at such contempt for the law and the Gardaí, not mentioning the contempt for himself, the judge exercised his powers by firm application of a record stiff fine.

GENUINE ALIBI

There was a particular judge who was infamous for being very bad tempered on the bench from time to time. All would suffer his wrath for the day if he was the worse for wear, having been drinking the night before. The immediate indicator for experienced Gardaí and solicitors was whether his face was very red or not. Red certainly meant danger!

I was in his court one day when he came out and sat on the bench. His face was red and the look on his face could cut ice. It was going to be a long day I thought.

During the various cases, mobile phones rang, cases were called and witnesses were not immediately available as they had to be called from smoking outside the court. There were regular interruptions with movement of people going in and out of a squeaky door and people were talking loudly at the back of the court. It was clear that all these distractions bothered the judge, but amazingly, he just stopped talking momentarily each time and held in his frustration and annoyance before proceeding again with determination.

Eventually, he could take no more! He stopped proceedings and began his speech with a barely controlled tone of volcanic anger.

"I have presided over cases in some of the worst courts throughout this country over the years. I can say without contradiction, that of all the courts in towns and cities I have worked in, I have never been treated with such contempt as I have been subjected to in this God-forsaken place."

He went on,

"You swan in and out of here as if it is a train station. Your mobile phones go off and there is the constant noise of you all talking loudly, as if you were in the pub."

Just then, while the judge was in the middle of his raving condemnation, a well-known local criminal and regular visitor to court, gets up from his seat and starts making his way towards the squeaky exit door. The judge stops his flow of speech and shouts down at him,

"And you, where do you think you are going?"

The criminal stops, faces the judge and without a thought, places his hands in front of his crotch area and for further emphasis, straightens his back, spreads his legs apart and unapologetically replies,

"I am going for a piss!"

Everyone - the public, Gardaí, defendants and solicitors - buried their faces in their hands to smother the nervous laughter that if detected, could see them face seven days in prison for contempt of court.

The judge simply pointed in the direction of the individual, shook his head, and then threw his arms up despondently over his head and shouted,

"I rest my case."

NO PREVIOUS CONVICTIONS

There are a few very basic rules of law in giving evidence when prosecuting in court. One is that details of previous convictions against a defendant cannot be given to the judge and jury, until a finding of guilt is declared. It is only when considering sentencing on conviction can the Garda give details of past cases the defendant has been convicted of. If a person has never been convicted of anything, the defending solicitor can, and usually does, make the judge and jury aware of it to help in mitigating the client's case.

The following story is a perfect example of why a person should let a solicitor defend you in court as against speaking up for yourself, DIY style.

There was an old man in a rural area who was suspected of making the illicit liquor, poteen, for years. Gardaí searched his home a number of times on warrant, but failed each time to find any evidence against him.

His luck finally ran out when an inquisitive Garda, in the course of a search, noticed a tap dripping liquid at the side of the chimney breast in the sitting room. The Garda initially thought it was a tap for the back boiler on the fire, but when he smelled the dripping liquid from the tap, the game was up.

The old man had a panelled wall beside the fireplace, behind which was the still, worm and bottles to gather the processed poteen. Ingenious!

The case came to court and the judge was presented with the evidence. The solicitor protested that his client had never, ever been in a court before in his life. He was of extremely good character, but for this one, singular indiscretion.

Before delivering his decision in the case the judge gave a lecture to the old man who was in the witness box.

"Do you know how many people have died, or were poisoned and ended up in hospital with serious liver complaints, as a direct result of homemade alcohol?"

Without a glance at his own solicitor, the old man immediately replied,

"For God's sake judge, I have been making good poteen for over thirty-five years and no one has ever died or got sick from it!"

All present, bar one, started howling in uncontrolled laughter, including the judge and the old man. The defending solicitor was not laughing as he sat down and buried his head in his hands.

The solicitor appeared to be the only one who fully grasped the consequences of the old man's confession!

IMPRESSING THE JUDGE

To be commended by a judge in court for good police work is a serious feather in the cap for an ambitious career-minded Garda. When considering awarding a Garda a Commissioner's written commendation for good police work much weight is given to a judge's favourable comments about a case in court.

One night while off duty I was in my local bar and was edging through the crowd about to leave. As I passed a couple in conversation it was obvious to me that the lad was chatting up this girl. I smiled to myself as I overheard the girl say to the lad,

"Hi, I'm Mary from Dun Laoire."

The way she said it had a somewhat poetic ring to it and it stuck in my mind.

Before I got to the door of the pub I met and struck up a conversation with a judge I knew well. We chatted for a while. I could see the girl I had passed earlier in the crowd, approach the bar counter. Mischievously, I said to the judge,

"I bet you I can have a good chat with the next stranger to come up to the bar beside us."

The judge looked at me with amusement and disbelief.

The girl stood at the bar, right beside the judge.

"Hi there," I said to the girl.

Somewhat defensively and cautiously the girl replied slowly,

"Hi."

The judge was looking at me with an expression of failure.

"*It's Mary, is it not?*" I said.

This partially disarmed the girl as she warmly replied yes with a confused expression on her face.

"*Mary from Dun Laoire, right?*"

Now her guard was completely down and she began chatting, enquiring how I knew her and where had we met before. The judge chuckled to himself as he looked on.

About a month later an officer came into my office at work. This did not happen very often.

"*God, Meehan, I was talking to the judge the other day after court and he was singing your praises,*" the officer said with amazement.

"*Really?*" I said.

"*Yeah, he said you had one very specific and admirable attribute!*"

"*What was that?*" I asked enthusiastically.

Smirking as he headed towards the door, he quipped,

"*He said you sure know how to chat up the women.*"

That was the only praise I ever got from a judge. Unfortunately, it could not be written up on my personnel file as a commendation for good police work!

CHAPTER 8
BIZARRE STORIES

Some of the stories in this final chapter
cannot fit easily into the category of blue humour
as they involve victims.
Black humour might be more appropriate.
To quote a famous politician
following a very strange series of incidents,
"Grotesque, unbelievable, bizarre, unprecedented."
The following stories are certainly GUBU!

THROWING 'LIGHT' ON THE SITUATION

I heard the desperate and frantic appeal for assistance over the radio by colleagues on my unit who were out on foot patrol. They were struggling with a man covered in petrol or some form of accelerant who was trying to set himself on fire.

I was on car patrol so I made it to the scene within a couple of minutes. My colleagues were wrestling on the pavement with this man who smelled like a petrol can. The man was resisting violently. Fuel was splashed over the pavement and nearby, a jumper was on fire on the ground. One of my colleagues, busy trying to restrain his arms and legs, shouted at me to get the cigarette lighter from the man's clenched fist.

The man's hand was very slippery because of the accelerant and I had great difficulty trying to stop him flicking the lighter. Eventually, I managed to wrench the lighter from his fist, pin him to the ground with my colleagues and handcuff him before whisking him off to hospital. The Fire Brigade was called out to hose the pavement and a nearby telephone box with chemical foam.

Back at the Garda Station my colleagues and I changed out of our petrol-soiled clothes. We spoke about the incident and thought of how lucky we were that the jumper that was on fire or the cigarette lighter had not ignited the petrol on the man or on the pavement.

"Sure the cigarette lighter must have been faulty or else had no fuel," I said.

I took the lighter and flicked it. It lit up, first time. We looked at each other in silence, our faces white with shock. All we could do was assume that the accelerant had dampened the lighter flint and made it difficult to strike a spark at the time. Sitting in my pocket after I seized it from the man it obviously dried out with the heat of my body.

A close call and a lucky break, to say the least!

COLD CASE

I got called to a burglary at a rented house one time. College students had returned to their pad and found it completely wrecked. Clothing had been stuck down the toilet, flooding the place and light fittings were pulled from the ceilings, among other things.

However, the worst act was that one of the burglars had defecated, placed it on a dinner plate and put the plate in the students' fridge. Thankfully, I later caught up with this individual and took him through the courts.

The *Phoenix* magazine subsequently got details of the case in the local newspapers and published it.

The heading they used for the article was appropriately, *Crap Visitors!*

TO ARREST OR NOT TO ARREST

I was at home in bed asleep when the door bell rang at three in the morning. With my eyes barely open, I got up and answered the door. There before me was a parent of a local criminal I had arrested a number of times. The parent was accompanied by a young man, unrelated, who I had also previously arrested for crime and drink-driving.

I knew by their demeanour that they were troubled about something and invited them into my home. They told me of their situation which was to immediately become my dilemma and problem.

The parent's son's girlfriend was pregnant and later that morning at six o'clock, they intended travelling to Britain to have an abortion. The people before me did not want this abortion to go ahead. They pleaded with me to arrest the young man I had dealt with so many times in the past.

I was faced with a very sensitive situation - about individual rights, the right to travel, the right to life, not to mention any thought of criminal law, religious or moral considerations. Whatever drowsiness I had felt from being half asleep quickly disappeared as I wondered what to do.

Before the parent and the young man left my house they gave me details of the couple's travel times and mode of transport. I said I would take time alone to think about what action I would take.

In the end, I was lucky that my personal decision was replaced by an unrelated legal responsibility. I was aware that there was a warrant to arrest in existence for this young man.

In law, I am duty bound to immediately execute such a warrant if I am made aware of the whereabouts of a person named in such a legal document. Two and a half hours later I was dressed and went to the Garda Station. One of the lads at work immediately knew I should not be working that tour and thought I had read the duty roster incorrectly. I made him none the wiser as he laughed at the supposed fool who had come to work in error at half-five in the morning thinking he was rostered for overtime. I grabbed a spare patrol car and went to a location along the road that I knew the van with the couple heading for the ferry would pass.

Within minutes the van arrived and I set up a checkpoint. The girl was in the front and her partner was hiding in the back. I arrested him and took him to the station. He was later before the courts and remanded in custody for a number of weeks. The trip was scuttled, as was the abortion, a direct consequence of my actions.

The child was born and is now a young adult.

What would you have done if you were in my shoes?

THE BATTLE OF THE BULGE!

A Garda supervisor always knows when a Garda is in trouble or is having difficulty in his/her work. On a day to day basis, Guards will call their supervisory Sergeant informally by their first name, particularly if the public are not within earshot. But when in trouble or in a situation out of their league, the Guard will invariably use the more formal greeting, 'Sergeant,' rather than the person's first name.

Disclosure of a problem usually starts with,

"Eh... Sergeant... Can I speak to you about something?"

And so it was one night in the Garda station. Garda John Vaughan had brought in a drunken driver and was in the Medical Room along with a local doctor processing the prisoner.

I was out in the main public office talking to another colleague. I began to wonder why a normally fairly speedy process was taking so long when Garda Vaughan eventually came out looking very serious and said,

"Sergeant, can you come in here please?"

I braced myself for the unknown. When I entered the Medical Room I saw a puddle of water on the ground. The prisoner was standing over it with a great big wet stain on his pants in the crotch area. He had some sort of a bulge in his pants half-way down his leg and he was smiling.

The doctor was sitting with his elbow on the table, supporting his head with his hand under his chin. He looked to be somewhere between boredom and frustration. Unlike the prisoner, he was not smiling. Neither was Garda Vaughan.

Then Garda Vaughan spoke in a very officious voice to me, in the presence of all,

"Sergeant, I strongly suspect that the prisoner put water instead of his urine into the jug!"

There was a jug sitting on the table immediately in front of the doctor and it had a small amount of liquid in it.

"Right. Doctor, are you satisfied that the liquid in the jug is the prisoner's urine?" I said.

"That's not urine," he said as he lifted his head from his hand and stuck his middle finger into the liquid and put it up to my face.

I will never know whether the doctor expected me to smell his finger, lick it or feel the temperature to confirm it was not in fact urine!

I searched the prisoner and found that the bulge in his pants was in fact a small plastic bottle. The prisoner was a regular drunken driver.

Later, he admitted to me that for years he carried a plastic bottle full of water in his underwear whenever he was out drinking. If arrested he could flick the water, instead of the urine, into the jug for analysis - an ingenious idea in theory, but only if performed while sober.

Sometime, when drunk, try to take a cap from a small bottle between your legs, through a narrow zipper, using one hand, while holding a jug in the other hand and all the time, under the scrutiny of other people! Impossible!

AT THE WRONG FUNERAL

There is almost nothing more tragic for a uniform police officer to deal with than a fatal traffic accident. The victim is often in the prime of life and health one minute; the next minute they are needlessly dead, along a lonely, silent, stretch of road.

The investigating Garda will have the most difficult of tasks in notifying the deceased relatives and bringing them to the morgue for identification of the dead person. This is not to mention getting to know the families very well later on throughout the process which includes taking statements, preparing investigation files, inquest evidence and maybe a prosecution court day.

Years later, it sometimes has to be revisited by all involved if an insurance claim has to be dealt with in the High Court. There is obviously nothing humorous about these cases, but the following story is bizarre to say the least and had a happy ending, for at least one family.

A colleague of mine had a call to respond to a fatal traffic accident. It was a pedestrian who was thumbing a lift at the side of the road and was hit by a passing car. At the scene, someone told my colleague that the victim was a local middle-aged single man who regularly thumbed a lift along the particular stretch of road. The body was brought to the hospital morgue escorted by Gardaí.

Family members were contacted and given the bad news. A relative of the deceased man arrived and, although shocked and grief stricken, went through the legal procedure of identifying the disfigured body. With a nod of the head the grieving relative acknowledged the body to be that of a specific relative.

A few days later my colleague called to his off-duty supervising Sergeant.

"Sergeant, we have a problem," he said.

In the course of the wake, prior to the funeral, the middle aged 'victim' had apparently walked into his home where all the relatives and sympathisers were waking his remains. He asked the speechless, shocked crowd, what all the commotion was about!

It turned out that this man who lived alone, had thumbed a lift to go on a three-day religious retreat in a nearby city, without telling anyone. The poor unidentified individual who had been killed was very similar in appearance to the man in question. The deceased man was, in fact, a 'knight of the road.' He was a homeless man of no fixed abode, who travelled throughout the whole country thumbing lifts, often sleeping in sheds or hostels.

CROSS BORDER INITIATIVE

A couple on holidays from the top of Northern Ireland were touring around Donegal. They visited Letterkenny town. After doing some shopping they returned to their car in Dillon's car park and then realised that they had locked their keys inside the car and could not get access.

It is a common misconception by the public that all Gardaí have equipment at their disposal to gain access to locked cars, similar to car thieves. It is not the case, but that said, individual members pride themselves in being able to do just that. It's all about trial and error and eventually one gets good at opening different makes of cars for stranded motorists. It becomes somewhat of a challenge.

The call came for us to go to the car park and assist the couple from Northern Ireland. I eventually managed to get the car open for them and they were most thankful. After a short general conversation we parted company, not before wishing them a good holiday.

A week later a *Thank You* card arrived at the Garda station, addressed to:
The Red Haired Mayo Garda,
Garda Station,
Letterkenny,
Co. Donegal.

I found this amusing and at some point told the story to my brother who lives in my home town of Westport in Mayo.

Over ten years later, my brother rang me one day. He told me that the night before while out socialising in a local bar in Westport, he had met up with a nice couple from Northern Ireland, whom he struck up a conversation with.

In the course of their conversation he asked if they were from Donegal, as he could not exactly place their accents. No, they explained, they were from further north, the other side of the border. My brother went on to explain that the only area he knew well enough up north was Letterkenny, as he visited a brother there sometimes.

"Ah, Letterkenny," said the lady, "we visited there many years ago, remember?"

"That's the place where we locked the keys into our car and had to get the police to open it," said her husband in reply.

My brother quizzed them further.

"By any chance was the Guard red-haired?"

"Yes," she said with amazement.

"And was he from Mayo by any chance?" asked my brother.

"Do you know what, you are absolutely correct, but how could you know that?" she asked.

"That was my brother!" he replied.

Small world indeed!

LOST PROPERTY

Garda records of any stolen item are captured on official computer and paper records, under the heading 'Stolen Property.' This covers every conceivable thing from a camera, mobile phone, TV, bicycle or cash to whatever one can imagine!

It certainly was not envisaged that it would be ever used to log an actual stolen property - a house! Imagine, a permanent building structure gone!

A newly promoted Sergeant took up duty at a very small rural station. On his very first day, a member of the public called to him at the station, enquiring impatiently, as to the current status of the investigation into his previously reported stolen property.

The Sergeant enquired as to what type of property had been stolen from him. The reply was,

"My house!"

The victims in this case had a holiday home and when they returned to their holiday property after a considerable absence, to their utter horror they discovered that the house was gone! Not a trace!

It turned out from investigations that the house had been completely bulldozed. There was a local grievance over the site and the matter ended up in a civil court case.

SMART PHONE...

Before the advent of mobile phones I had a confidential source I could ring anytime to get help with solving a crime. The source was very contactable for a time, even though there was neither a land-line nor a mobile phone in the home!

He was really the first person ever to possess a smart phone!

So you are wondering how I could make phone contact with my source so easily! The source lived in a caravan, parked right up against a public phone box. When it rang and no one else was obviously nearby awaiting a call, the source knew the call was ringing for them.

It's one novel way to avoid land line rental costs or mobile phone charges!

ALL QUIET ON THE WESTERN FRONT

Before computerisation any Garda finishing patrol had to complete a written log of their duty in a register called a Patrol Book. In this record one would have to write a summary of the activities completed during a tour. Among these were the areas patrolled, the number of arrests, premises checked for security lock-up, sightings of suspects and serious incidents dealt with.

On a quiet night if there were few incidents, it became so routine that members documented it with the same old jargon, like a repeated poem of the duties and activities carried out. That said, it was checked each morning by the Sergeant in charge of the station and anything of note would be brought to the attention of the Superintendent.

One night in Castlebar it had been a quiet night and a Garda who should have been patrolling the town had opted to spend the entire tour of duty inside the station catching up on paperwork and files. At the end of the tour, he filled in the Patrol Book with the usual list of checked this, patrolled this area and that, and ended the fictitious log with, *"All quiet, nothing unusual to report."*

At six in the morning the Garda in question finished duty and left the station to drive home. Along one of the streets he saw an old decommissioned light aeroplane, minus its wings, parked neatly like a car. The wingless plane had been transported from the local airport by someone and temporarily parked up on the street for some reason.

The Guard had to rush back to the station, take out the Patrol Book and write an addendum to his report, *"All quiet, nothing unusual to report... other than an aeroplane parked on one of the streets!"*

HOW CAN SOMETHING SO BAD TURN OUT SO GOOD?

The message came to us by radio while on mobile patrol, *"Report of burglary in progress at a house in Urseline Crescent."* The unidentified good citizen who had called in the crime in progress had even given the specific house number. We raced to the scene and arrived at the entrance to the housing estate within a few minutes.

We saw a suspicious looking young man walking quickly out of the housing estate and we decided to check him out. We asked him for identification and the purpose of his movements so late at night. He was uneasy but on being searched had nothing illegal on his person. Satisfied as to his identity, we let him go and continued through the estate to the house reportedly being burgled.

When we arrived we found the house to be completely secure, with no sign of illegal entry or damage. We knocked on the door a number of times, but there was no reply. No one came near us not even the 'neighbour' who had phoned in to us.

After some time checking around the place, we decided it must have been yet another hoax call. We left the area to deal with a backlog of other calls.

The following morning all hell broke loose. We were told by members of the station crime unit that a burglary had taken place at the house number reported and not only was property stolen, the sitting room was set on fire and some damage caused before the fire service arrived and put the fire out.

It turned out the burglary was at Ursuline Court not Ursuline Crescent. These two estates are back to back and there is only a pedestrian access between them.

We had either been given the wrong estate address by the control room or we had picked it up wrongly at the other end of the radio. Either way, it was most embarrassing and disappointing. The owner of the house was furious when she heard that a neighbour had contacted the Gardaí and they had apparently failed to respond.

The absentee landlord/owner of the vacant house, or should I say, the victim of this crime, rang me at work and gave me a proper ear full. I was totally apologetic and tried, without success, to explain to her what had occurred.

She was not listening and said she had lost complete faith in us as a police force. I said that I really regretted this and would do everything in my power to sort things out. The call ended with the victim hanging up on me.

All was not lost however! We had a suspect and there was more urgency than most cases to sort this one out. The youth we had stopped at the wrong estate was picked up and interviewed and eventually admitted the crime.

It turned out he had fled the scene from one estate and had taken the pedestrian walkway through the other estate to avoid being detected by responding Gardaí. Because we had gone to the wrong estate we had luckily met him. Had we responded by going to the correct estate we would not have met the fleeing thief going in the opposite direction. That said, he admitted that he had heard our speeding car approaching him and had hidden a television and video behind shrubbery before we confronted him.

I let the crime unit deal with the case from this point on as I was advised by them that the victim was in no mood to deal with the specific Gardaí who had failed her.

Months later, out of the blue, I get this call at work. It was from the lady victim of the same crime. She was almost crying with emotion.

She began apologising for her previous attitude on the phone to me and was seeking my forgiveness.

We spent some time apologising to each other and asking each other for forgiveness. It turned out, with the passage of time and successful conviction of the culprit in court, a colleague from the crime unit had explained the full story to her. Her faith in the police had been restored, if not enhanced.

A GAS 'TICKET'

The story goes that a group of young country lads went up to an All-Ireland GAA match in Dublin many years ago. After the match when they returned to their car which was parked along the Quays, they found a big dirty parking ticket on the windscreen wiper.

A rough-looking dodgy character walked past the lads as they were standing there giving out about the parking fine they had received.

The unknown youth interrupted the lads' conversation and said that for £20 he could promise that the ticket would not result in a fine. He was confident that he could make it - disappear!

Although extremely dubious about this individual's confidence, curiosity as well as hope compelled them to hand over the money.

Without further hesitation or explanation, the youth rushed away. The last they saw of this individual was the sight of him running past the traffic warden, swiping the ticket book from his hands and flinging it into the River Liffey, before sprinting away into the distance.

A gas 'ticket' of a man you might say!

SLOW DEATH

A member of the public had found an emaciated dog at the side of the road. It was so thin its ribs were showing and it was so weak that it was almost unable to walk, let alone breathe. It was evident to all that it needed to be put down immediately to relieve it from further pain and discomfort. Who gets the call? Not a vet or animal shelter, we did!

That time, each station was issued with a humane killer for such cases. It was a small single-barrel weapon with a large brass cone-shaped cup at the end which was placed against the head of the animal. A bullet was put in the other end sealed behind a cap. A hammer was provided to strike a firing pin to shoot a bullet down the barrel and into the head of the animal to be killed.

Garda Moerton and I had never used this contraption before but it looked easy enough. The dog was in the rear garden of the house of the good public-spirited woman who reported the dog's plight to us. She was so upset and was relieved to see us, but then left us alone to get on with the job. Unknown to us at the time, she was waiting at the front of her house for the sound of the bullet which would signal the end of the poor dog's pain.

I quickly put a bullet in the contraption and disposed of the poor animal. No doubt the lady at the front of the house heard the shot and was relieved. Garda Moreton said to me,

"I never used one of those things. Can I have a go?"

"Sure," I said.

In the next few minutes the contraption was loaded up again and Garda Moreton put another round into the already dead dog. The lady heard the shot and jumped with shock. The dog is still not dead and it had suffered a second bullet before it died, she would have thought.

"I wonder what range the humane killer has?" I said to Garda Morton.

"Let's see," said he and we put another round in the gun and aimed it at a tree some distance away in the garden.

Bang! A shot rings out for the third time in almost half an hour and a lady at the front of the house is almost having a nervous breakdown and in need of sedation!

Real tactful Gardaí in action!

DOG GONE

There was a disturbance by a large number of youths at Market Square, Letterkenny late one night. They were mainly shouting loud and drinking from cans. We arrived and advised them to keep the noise down. Drink cans hidden behind shrubbery were unceremoniously poured down the roadside drain by us in front of the youths. No one complained or claimed ownership of the drink as they were mostly underage.

One of the group had a big angry looking dog and the youth holding it threatened to set it on us. The dog barked viciously at us and took up an attack stance in response to the orders of its master.

My colleague simply walked forward without any fear, grabbed the big dog by the scruff of the neck and hindside, and roared at me to open the boot of the car. Suddenly, there was silence all round as the boot of the car closed and we began to leave the area. As we left, the dog owner called us everything under the sun and said,

"Take it away! I couldn't give a f***, it's not mine."

We brought the animal to the local dog pound and thought no more about it.

A few days later, I was on duty at the public desk in the station when the previously aggressive loud-mouthed youth who owned the dog came in. He was meeker than before and his body language was somewhat less challenging.

"I am here to get my dog back," he said.

Taking delight in having this guy squirm and backtrack somewhat from our previous encounter, I said,

"I thought you said you didn't own the dog and to quote you, 'I couldn't give a f***, it's not mine.'"

160

"No," he said, impatiently, *"I want my dog back."*

Having pushed it enough and having first given him a lecture about his bad behaviour, I agreed to let it be and rang the dog pound in his presence. I enquired from the staff as to the procedure, including the possible cost, of releasing the dog.

Across the phone came the reply from the staff member of the dog shelter,

"That dog was put down here yesterday."

When I told the young fella the situation, he all but controlled his quivering lower lip and possible tears as he once again called me everything under the sun. He left the station in a storm of fury, slamming the door behind him, almost taking it from its hinges. I genuinely felt sorry for the guy and his dog, at least for a while anyway.

A week or two later, while I was on mobile patrol, I happened to drive past the 'ex-dog owner.' On seeing me, he immediately started roaring all sorts of abuse and had no difficulty giving a long string of abusive names for us without needing to repeat a single curse.

My response to this confrontation was one which would have been expected of any tactful, professionally trained police officer in such a trying situation! I stuck my head out the window and repeatedly growled back at him,

"Bow, wow! Bow, wow! Grrrr... "

It's what we call, in community policing jargon, 'winning hearts and minds!'

QUICK RECOVERY

I worked with a Guard who was normally very cranky but who sometimes surprisingly showed a more soft, compassionate side to his nature.

A young college student came into a Garda Station one day in a very distressed state. His bicycle had just been stolen in the city centre and he was almost in tears.

Overhearing this report being dealt with by another Garda, Mr Cranky interrupted,

"Follow me, young man," he said.

The student followed my colleague without saying anything through the various hallways of the station before arriving at an outdoor locked shed at the rear of the station. The student wondered to himself how his bike could have been recovered by the Guards so quickly. It had only been stolen a few minutes before he had called to the station!

In the shed were hundreds of bicycles which had been recovered by the Gardaí or handed into the Station by members of the public when found abandoned.

"Do you see your bike in that lot, young man?" Cranky said.

"No sir," said the student.

An angry frown came on my colleague's face, which the student immediately detected. My colleague then said to the student in an impatient, cross voice, winking at him at the same time,

"Take another good look and tell me if you see your bike in there, or a bike which is similar to yours."

The student, now clearly uncomfortable, looked again and said bravely,

"No, I cannot see my bike, but, but, ... it was somewhat similar to that bike over there!"

My colleague's face lit up and the frown suddenly disappeared.

"Good man, that's your bike!" he said confidently.

"No, no, I just said it looks similar to my bike," said the student quickly, so as not to be misinterpreted.

Although obviously an intelligent person, the student was very slow to read the signals of the unorthodox generosity being offered by my colleague.

The frown returned to the face of my colleague. He moved closer to the student and in an intimidating stance, said in a low, slow, angry and accusing voice,

"Is that your bike there, young man?"

Realising that 'no' was not the acceptable answer, he replied,

"Possibly."

"Good man. Good man," said my colleague with glee, pointing to the rear exit gate.

"Take YOUR bike now young man and good luck to you."

The nervous but relieved young student then left the yard with 'his' bike.

All is well that ends well!

NO MORE HEROES ANYMORE

The call came to the station that there was a potential 'jumper' (a person attempting suicide by jumping off a bridge) on the outskirts of the town. Gardaí and the Fire Service raced to the scene. On arrival, I could see a man down in the fast flowing river. He appeared to be pinned to the wall of the bridge, no doubt due to the pressure of the strong current against him.

The Fire Brigade was there ahead of me and many of the firemen were standing on the ditch of the river near the bridge. I was wondering what the delay was in carrying out a rescue. I moved closer and heard the Fire Chief order each of his crew members in turn to go in and get the person out of the water. In turn, each and every one of the fire man firmly replied,

"No. Not me!"

Unaware of the full facts at the time, I was baffled, disgusted, and yet if it was not so serious a matter, it would almost be a comedy I was witnessing. I said to them that I was going into the water.

"No," insisted the Fire Chief, before pointing to one of the firemen and saying, *"Jimmy Joe, you are ordered to go in, as you have the waterproofs already on."*

"No," replied Jimmy Joe, the fireman, *"I went in after him last week and the time before that too!"*

I later learned that this man had gone to the bridge so many times before, that all the poor firemen on the unit had gone into the cold water and rescued him. Some had done so several times. The guy, alive and well today, was obviously rescued by the firemen again that night in question, as on all previous occasions.

IN THE WRONG BEDROOM

A very drunk man returned to his home in an estate after a night on the beer. He was so drunk he had difficulty finding his home as it was in a row of similarly designed houses.

Eventually, he found his home, but had so much difficulty putting the key in the door and opening it that he became violent. Due to his impatience, he put his fist through the glass in the door and opened it from the inside lock lever. He immediately went upstairs, stripped naked and went to bed.

A short time later, we had a call from a concerned resident of the same estate. The public spirited person reported the sound of breaking glass at a nearby house and suspected a burglary was in progress. On our arrival, we found the house with the damaged door and went inside to investigate. Upstairs we found the drunken man in bed in a deep sleep.

This was not a burglary, just a drunken man, not only in the wrong bed room, but also in the wrong house. He lived a few doors down the estate!

NOT IN NEED OF PUBLIC ASSISTANCE WITH THIS PARTICULAR CASE

Throughout my career I had, more than once, to negotiate with unfortunate people in the process of attempting suicide. On one such occasion, I was trying to talk down a young man from jumping off a bridge. It was after three o'clock in the morning and there was a lot of passing taxi traffic bringing drunken revellers home from the various local night clubs and late bars.

I was doing well with calming down and persuading the young individual not to jump. Suddenly, some drunken fool passing by in a taxi roared out the window,

"Go on you coward, jump."

The distressed individual hanging over the bridge, clinging to nothing more than a fence rail, immediately asked me in an agitated loud voice,

"What did that person just say?"

I knew the enormity telling the truth would have on the already over distressed man, so I replied with a white lie,

"He said you are a coward... if you jump!"

That drunken plonker in the taxi could have easily caused the young man to literally tip over the edge by his grossly inappropriate remark.

Thankfully, the distressed individual was later safely escorted from the bridge, given appropriate help and is in a better frame of mind to this day.

The End

ACKNOWLEDGEMENT

I wish to sincerely thank and give whole-hearted appreciation to Liamy Mac Nally of Covie Publications and Recordings (CPR) who was so genuinely positive about this project from the very outset and kept me believing. The professionalism in the manner in which he proofread the draft and made much-needed recommendations about print layout was tremendous. Liamy was energetically available to discuss the project at any time, even if it cost me a lot of coffee at Christy's Harvest café in Westport! Besides the professional side of things, on a personal level, Liamy is simply a great person.

I equally owe a great debt of gratitude to graphic artist and illustrator Pat Tracey of Hand Eye Studios. I have always been an admirer of his work. We grew up in the same neighbourhood, but little did I know that one day we would work together on a book and that I would have the honour of being associated with his talented artistic abilities. Pat was always a pleasure to work with and we just laughed and joked our way through each meeting as we came up with various ideas for cartoons for stories in the book. I think you will agree that his work on the book cover speaks volumes about the talent of this man.

In summary, Pat, like Liamy, made this journey a joy rather than a labour. I salute you both and take my (police) hat off in acknowledgement of your contribution.

Cyril Meehan